REAL
ationships

Navigating our world of complex connections

Richard Beaumont

What others have said about REALationships

Murray Baird

www.murraybaird.com

Legal Practitioner and advisor on the Law, Governance and Regulation of Charities. Timid sailor and friend.

"This REALationships book is easy to read but hard to live. It captures lasting principles in real-life examples from Richard's keen observations of life. His sailing examples take you to all points of the compass and the notes pages make you think about your own voyage. Whether you are sailing downwind with sails filled or beating up-wind under stormy skies, this book will keep you on course."

Jason T Smith

www.jasontsmith.com.au

Thought-leader, author, speaker & founder of the Back In Motion Health Group.

"Richard *lives* his message. As one who is so widely travelled, experienced and accomplished in life, it is clear that one of Richard's greatest discoveries is the importance of relationship and connection with people. I am a fortunate beneficiary of his friendship. Richard has the remarkable quality of making you feel like the most important and valued person in the room when he stops to talk with you. From this place of authenticity, his words in this book carry enormous authority. Richard's life inspires me to love people more, and REALationships shows you how."

Matt Bird,

CEO of Relationology International

"REAL is one of the best books I have read about how to build genuine relationships. If you would like to 'stop networking and start relationships' then this book is a must read."

Moses Lim

What The Green CEO/Founder

"REALationships is a thought-provoking book that challenges the common worldly concepts of relationships and leadership. It encapsulates skills and tips to navigate challenges at all levels of life with wisdom, learnt over a lifetime of being a servant leader."

REAL
ationships

Navigating our world of complex connections

by

Richard Beaumont

Published by RB

Copyright © Richard Beaumont 2020

The moral right of the author has been asserted.

First Published in 2020

This edition published in 2020

Author: Richard Beaumont

Title: REALationships

ISBN: 9780648980605

Cover Design: by Ogsaint

Book Design: by Daniel - Global Desing

All rights reserved. No part of this publication may be reproduced or transmitted in any form or by any means, electronic or mechanical, including photocopying, recording or any information storage or retrieval system, without prior permission in writing from the publisher.

The publisher has no control over, or responsibility for, any third-party websites referred to or in this book. All internet addresses given in this book were correct at the time of going to press. The author and publisher regret any inconvenience caused if addresses have changed or sites have ceased to exist and can accept no responsibility for any such changes.

RB Publishing
PO Box 553
Doncaster
Victoria 3128
AUSTRALIA

Website: www.richardbeaumont.com.au
Email: rb@richardbeaumont.com.au
LinkedIn: Richard Beaumont
Facebook: Richard Beaumont

ISBN: 9780648980605

To my incredible wife Julie.

Loving, caring, patient, long-suffering and supportive of all I do.

Forever grateful!

Preface

I had no intention of writing a book. But here it is anyway! It came about as a result of several converging REALationships in my life. Many friends encouraged me to give others the opportunity to learn some of the insights I have gained, in order to share the benefits with them.

I have been to a lot of places and experienced more than most would see in two lifetimes! I love telling stories and exposing those I connect with, to the often harsh realities of life I regularly encounter when working in developing nations. I am a life-long learner and my passion is not only to grow more as an individual, but also help others find fulfilment in whatever they do. I want readers to understand that real fulfillment in life comes through realationships.

That deep inner satisfaction everyone is seeking is not found in more money, a faster car, a beautiful home, a luxurious boat, a successful career, jetting around the world, or even public recognition. I have experienced a measure of all these things. I have experienced true contentment in grounded open, caring, engaging, giving relationships. The solid foundation of my life is found in my realationship with our creator. You may have a different faith, belief or life-philosophy to me - or none at all, but regardless of how you live and whatever you choose to believe, the principles I have outlined in this book will help you achieve those sought-after realationships for yourself.

My good friend Lindsay Clarke, (www.mclubonline.com) was the first person to help me understand the significant level of expertise I had gained over many years in the area of relationships. His outstanding M-Club

Leadership Course guided, prodded and stretched me into recognising the fact there was a book in me that needed to be shared with the world! Thank you Lindsay for helping me see it and coaching me to write it.

The actual writing process was surprisingly enjoyable. It didn't take long. This book was written over a period of six weeks, in six different countries. I started in Auckland, New Zealand while staying with my family. In spite of my brother Roger advising me to "leave out the reflection page" – I kept it anyway because I thought it would help the readers process what I have written and apply it to their own lives.!

Australia, Singapore, Myanmar, Laos and Thailand were the other locations where I reflected on my experiences and plugged away at my laptop. The book was imagined in hotels, airport departure lounges, on multiple flights and even on my friend Hom's little farm, an hours' drive from Vientiane, Laos. This quick ten day, four nation trip was to meet with the local partners we help fund through the foundation I work with.

The manuscripts 'first cut' was done by an experienced editor, Reinalyn Cabag (Yen) who lives in Iloilo in the Philippines. I almost got to meet Yen and her family, but it was right at the beginning of the Covid outbreak. It was possible to fly to Manilla, but it was not possible to leave! We have yet to meet. Thanks Yen for your collaboration, encouragement and great ideas, you helped me make sense of what I was endeavouring to communicate.

The 'comma police' is my affectionate description of kate Munns. Kate is one of the Entrust Foundation project managers on my team. If anything has slipped past Kate – it was me fiddling after she had completed her edit and passed on her many helpful suggestions! Kate your work is valued – thanks for making the book readable, relevant and still sound like me!

My good friend and sailing companion, Murray Baird often quoted the "sailing - a metaphor for life" analogy. Thanks Murray – I stole it. We have sailed on large and smaller yachts together. He is the more technical sailor and I am the more adventuresome. Murray gets nervous when we venture beyond the harbour, which is the point at which my adrenaline starts to kick in. I gave Murray a draft copy of this book so he could add an endorsement. In true realational style, he then kindly offered to edit it for me. I concluded that offer could only mean one thing. The manuscript was terrible! After asking him a couple of blunt questions, I was gently assured by Murray that New Zealanders regularly get their vowels wrong and it just needed a little tweaking! Consider it tweaked!

Murray thanks for your assistance, suggestions and pointers to a couple of my experiences I had shared with you over the years and your optimism that they would be a helpful inclusion. I believe the book is richer for your input. (Dinner is on me!)

CONTENTS

Introduction – Sailing, a metaphor for life.

PART ONE

How to implement relational change.

Step 1...**19**
Deciding to Go About: Changing direction in our relationships.
- Realational heroes who have impacted the world.
- Why are relationships such a struggle?
- Fake relationships? No thanks!

Step 2...**31**
Discarding the cookie cutter: Treating everyone as bespoke.
- Understanding the relationship spectrum.
- Levels of complexity.
- What are vertical relationships?

Step 3...**47**
Developing 'Selfie' awareness: How do others really see me?
- How do I see myself?
- What do they say when I am not there?
- Identifying my fundamental flaws.

Step 4...**61**
Don't touch that! Five realational 'No-Nos'
- Charger or drainer?
- Identifying the cringe factor.
- How to build trust.

Step 5...**85**
Inside Out! Delivering a fresh set of values.
- W.I.I.F.M.
- Symbiotic relationships.
- Seek first to understand…

Step 6...**103**
Determining your True North: Charting a wise course.
- The glue called coffee.
- Navigating the rocks of relationship.
- Where am I heading?

PART TWO
Becoming a Realational Leader.

Chapter 7..**121**
    Heart matters: The power of relational leadership.
- Five stages of communication.
- Life-traits of a successful follower.
- It is amazing how much can be achieved…

Chapter 8..**135**
    Seven secrets: Thriving team relations.
- Change of course required.
- Check the chart.
- Navigation by trust, accountability through realationship.

Chapter 9..**155**
    Effective. Authentic. Radical. A fresh approach to client relationships.
- Networking is 'old-school'.
- Swimming up-stream.
- Chasing a 'Win-Win'.

Chapter 10..**171**
    Shift happens: Agility and the speed of change.
- A wind shift.
- Checking conditions - adjusting our course.
- Non-negotiables in the midst of change.

Chapter 11..**181**
    Tacking into a head wind: Effort well rewarded.
- ust another "How to?"
- Effort invested will reward us well.
- Heading for Hobart.

Chapter 12..**193**
    Using your skills to streak ahead: Setting your spinnaker.
- The value of realationships.
- The deep satisfaction of helping others.
- Making our world a better place.

'Sailing – a metaphor for life.'

Life is not always smooth sailing.

I was born in Christchurch, New Zealand. I have never lived far from the sea. Summers were spent at the beach or near a river flowing straight off the Southern Alps – always cold and bracing. My parents insisted on swimming lessons to keep me safe and I have always thrived in or near water - swimming, surfing or crewing on my Uncle Jim's 40 foot yacht in Lyttleton Harbor.

My love of sailing was born at Redcliffs Sailing Club. Situated on the edge of a tidal estuary, just a few kilometres from Christchurch, the club boasted a flotilla of rundown boats perched precariously on the hard stand, adjacent to the estuary. The current runs in and out at a great rate of knots - dependent on time, tide and wind.

When I was 16 years old, I purchased a small Sabot sailing dingy—that's a sailing dinghy that you can sail and race single-handedly. I can't remember how much it cost but it was all of 2 metres long with a flattened bow and a tiny "P" class sail to drive it. I knew little of how to sail but was keen to give it my best shot.

In a light wind, I launched the sailing dingy on a departing tide and headed up the estuary on a broad reach. The sail filled with wind, the boat leaned over and the water rushed past. Wow! I was flying along – an expert already - and very excited! It was not until I glanced up at the bank of the estuary that I realized that, in fact, I was actually going backwards, being pushed out to sea. The current was running faster than the forward momentum of the dingy!

A close friend and fellow sailor regularly reminds me that sailing is a metaphor for life. Sometimes we think we are doing well flying along with our lives and having a wonderful time. But then something happens we do not expect. We are forced to stop, take stock and check the markers around us. It begins to dawn on us that in spite of all our effort and the excitement and activity around us, we are actually going backwards! The Covid-19 pandemic is a classic example.

The most challenging part of my life, and I am guessing yours, has been in the complex arena of relationships. How do we maintain our integrity, develop our businesses, build our teams, manage our family and maximise our social engagement while still maintaining deep meaningful, unselfish, vibrant, life-giving relationships?

I want this book to help us do just that. We will dig into and examine our motivation. How do we think, what is really important, how do we handle difficult people and how can we thrive while navigating our world of complex connections and relationships?

I have offered some questions for reflection at the end of each chapter. You might answer them on your own, or with a friend or partner. Use them to build your work team and increase your opportunities for success in your business.

I will use some sailing metaphors and my hope is that you learn a little more about the thrill and sometimes solitude of sailing. My motivation in writing this book is to help others not only learn about the value of relationships, but rather gain a true insight into what I have come to understand as REALationships.

Sailing – a metaphor for life. If on occasions we feel we are going backwards in our relationships, this book will give you the tools we need to help master the art of REALationships – in every area of our life. It will take us deeper, give us insights, tools and practical tips to take us further than we could ever imagine.

If we apply the insights and life experiences I share in this book, in our own lives, we can master our **real**ationships and our life journey will be an amazing ride. How can I be so confident of this? Because my life has been an amazing journey. Read on and find out how.

Richard Beaumont - November 2020

STEP 1

Deciding to *Go About*: Why we need to change direction in our relationships.

> *"I can't change the direction of the wind, but I can adjust my sails to always reach my destination."*
>
> - Jimmy Dean

"Prepare to go about," shouted Cameron, the skipper of the classic yacht, Bungoona. We were competing in a Sunday classic yacht race on Port Philip Bay in Melbourne, Australia. "Lee Ho" was the next shout we heard, which resulted in a flurry of activity. My task was to hold the main sheet tight in the wooden cleat until the boat went through the eye of the wind. The boat changed direction and the wind was coming from the other side of the sail so that it was whipped to the other side of the cockpit. This was followed by me rapidly pulling on a rope, wrapping it around the adjacent port winch and making the sail as tight as possible - without losing any of boat speed that we had achieved.

"Hurry up," growled Cameron, "we don't want to lose our place." He later admitted it was a good tack. A satisfied skipper is something of value to a humble deck hand.

'Going about' is a sailing term that means we are changing direction. This manoeuvre is undertaken while doing all we can to maintain a forward momentum. Throughout life, we need to be willing to change what we have been doing and start to see things differently all while continuing to move forward. We change course, and therefore direction, without losing momentum.

The Jimmy Dean quote (at the beginning of this chapter) is an accurate description of a successful life. We can't change the headwinds that affect us and drive us. We can't change the pressures of life and business that seek to push us in multiple directions, often at the same time. But we *can* adjust our course by choosing the direction we wish to go. If we are intentional about our direction, how we set our sails, how often we *'go about'* – we will eventually reach our desired destination.

This principle applies to multiple aspects of our lives: our education, what we choose to learn, whether we attend university, our career path, our life partner, the country in which we live, and the integrity we demonstrate in all aspects of our lives. What about the goals we set, the *"stuff"* we accumulate, the way we want others to see us and the way we see others? All these things shape the course of our lives and will ultimately determine the sort of life we choose for ourselves and share with those we love.

I have learned that quality relationships lie at the heart of everything we seek to do in our lives. If we can thrive in our relationships - including the difficult ones - I believe we can thrive in our lives. Everyone knows a difficult person and I'm sure everyone reading this book could easily write down a list of them!

REALationships

The problem we all face is that relationships have grown more complicated in this age of internet visibility. Public figures, who have always lived their lives in a goldfish bowl, are in the limelight more than ever. Everyone sees what they do and who they do it with. In the 21st century, we are all experts at deciding whether they have done the right thing, spent their money the right way, made the wisest decisions or raised their family well. However, what we see online does not show us how they really deal with their relationships behind the scenes.

I know many people I would describe as **Real**ational heroes. This recognition is based on the way they have developed, maintained and maximised the depth of relationships they have built over the years. More importantly, it's about how they have developed their relationships and what they have achieved in making our world a better place - looking out for others, changing nations, running governments, supporting the underdogs and marginalised, standing alongside the poorest people on the planet and enabling them to lead a better life. Making it possible for their fellow humans, struggling to get a simple start, to get a handhold on the bottom rung of the ladder of life.

Bill Gates, founder of Microsoft, was the richest man in the world at 39 years old. The 'Bill and Melinda Gates Foundation' was established in 2000 when Bill and his wife set up an organisation to support philanthropic work in more than 100 countries that faced challenges in education, poverty, hunger and health. They have given grants totalling over $50 million dollars (as of the end of 2018 - and counting). They do not do it remotely. They regularly visit the poorest – the very people they help. They connect real-ationally because that is the way they remain focused on the enormous task facing our world.

None of us can manage a business, a family or a foundation if we are remote from the coalface, from the people with whom we are working. We can only remain effective and focused in our endeavours if we are engaged in **Real**ationships.

> *"I believe the returns on investment in the poor are just as exciting as successes achieved in the business arena and they are even more meaningful!"*
>
> – BILL GATES

Another person I greatly admire is Nelson Mandela. Mandela was a South African anti-apartheid political leader who focused the early years of his life on dismantling the apartheid regime in South Africa. Mandela served 27 years in prison, spending some time on Robben Island – off the coast of Cape Town. He was released from prison in 1990 by the then President, FW de Klerk as a direct outcome of strong international and internal pressures.

Mandela joined with de Klerk to negotiate an end to apartheid. The result was that Nelson Mandela evolved from prisoner to president in the 1994 multi-racial general election. He became South Africa's first black head of state between 1994 – 1999.

I believe Mandela, although a controversial figure for much of his life, was a **real**ational hero. He was in a "no-win" situation. Critics on the political 'right' claimed he was a communist terrorist while those on the political 'left' denounced him as too eager to negotiate and reconcile with apartheid's supporters. He realised he could not please everyone but managed to navigate the treacherous waters of South African politics using his humility and **real**-ational skills, refined by 27 years of imprisonment. I see him as an icon of democracy and social justice, aptly rewarded the joint Nobel Peace Prize in 1993 along with FW de Klerk.

REALationships

> *"One of the things I learned when I was negotiating was that until I changed myself, I could not change others."*
>
> – NELSON MANDELA

Change does not always come about at university or when we are successful. In my experience, change comes about in adversity, when times are tough, when you feel vulnerable, when life isn't giving us what we would like – or expect. The tools of life are forged in the battles, during the times we feel we are in over our heads, when we don't know what to do next. **Real**ationships are the societal glue that enables us to survive and thrive during these times. When business or life is going well, ***real***ationships will be what drives this momentum and enables us to soar. When things are tough, ***real***ationships will be what gets us through the struggle and out the other side.

Another ***real***ational genius was Noelene Bertram Beaumont – a special person to me. She was my Mum. She was born with only one hand, her left arm ending at the wrist forming a stump. It never bothered me. As far as I was concerned it was always that way. During my childhood years I watched my mother raise five boys, run a busy household, entertain and feed the constant stream of house guests, manage life, drive a manual car, shop, garden, paint and decorate. Her disability did not stop her for once second. In fact, I came to realise that mum's disability possibly helped her develop a personality and charisma that engaged others in a unique way. It made her the love of everyone who had the privilege to meet her and get to know her.

Mum's personality meant that many people did not even notice her missing hand. She always showed such a keen interest in whoever she was talking to. She rarely talked about herself. If asked, she would always direct the conversation back to the other person. "Tell me about your family." "What is it that you love doing?" "What are you studying and how are you finding that?" "When did you two meet, and how is your friendship developing?"

When I was sixteen, I invited my latest girlfriend, Julie to a party that was being hosted at our family home in Christchurch, New Zealand. I thought it was a 'safe' event to bring Julie along to because there were 70 other young people there and I naively thought that Mum couldn't get to them all!

Helping clear up after most of the guests had gone home, my mother managed to connect with Julie. As people were leaving and the clean-up continued, my mother sat Julie down in a quiet corner of our lounge room. I remember looking across the room seeing the two of them together and thinking, "Oh my goodness, trouble ahead, Mum will find out way too much information from my new girlfriend!"

When recalling that incident and many subsequent conversations that took place, Julie recounts, "She was such an amazing person. She was always so interested in me, I often found myself telling her things that I shared with very few others!"

Julie is now my wife of 44 years and we regularly talk about Noelene with the fondest of memories: inquisitive, engaging, interested, not nosey, not intrusive, caring, and overall, an amazing realational woman.

As I reflect while writing this, it has dawned on me afresh just how strongly my life has been influenced by Noelene. For 40 years I watched, listened and learned from her - not as a student, but as one who was unknowingly being coached. I realise I have absorbed into my personality the way she lived her life, the way she managed her **real**ationships. It was an osmosis, an unconscious ingestion of her love for people, her gentle probing, while always displaying a genuine interest in others. That is how I learned to develop **real**ationships with an incredibly wide range of people. These **real**ationships are able to transcend culture, colour, religion, gender, class, sexual preference, education and age.

At this point you may have already decided, 'that skill level is not me.' You may feel that you can never be a Bill and Melinda Gates, a Nelson Mandela, or even a Noelene Beaumont. If we are honest, we all struggle with our relationships. It may be a work colleague, a boss, our CEO, a team member, the group for who we are responsible, our wives, husbands, partners, maybe an annoying friend, a noisy neighbour, our in-laws, out-laws – whoever! Few know how to thrive by truly understanding the secrets of developing **real**ationships.

Generational changes mean that we all see the world through a different lens. *'Boomers'* have a different would-view to *'Millennials.'* Friends in business tell me that they have some of the best educated, smartest people they know working for them. But they don't know how to talk to each other." They complain that "they know how to text or snapchat, but they don't know how to talk!" "I need to know how to help them engage at a meaningful level so they can help each other, work well within a team structure and achieve outstanding results for themselves and our business!"

This, I believe, is the lament of many business leaders. How do we help our people engage with each other – let alone clients – so our business can develop, grow and thrive?

We live in a culture influenced, partly, by leaders such as former US President Donald Trump, Kim Jong-un of North Korea, Nanendra Modi,

Prime Minister of India and Xi Jinping, leader of China. Each with their own agenda. Fake news has become an epidemic. Who do we believe? What is their spin? How do we identify their real agenda? In the year of Covid-19, Trump put his own 'spin' on the pandemic. China was blamed by the ever-present conspiracy theorists and Modi 'locked down' a country of 1.3billion people with barely four hours' notice!

I believe we live in an age of fake relationships. Twitter feeds, Facebook likes, LinkedIn connections, Snapchat photos, YouTube followers What are we actually measuring? How many of our Facebook friends do we really know? My research revealed that a new career has been developed by a group dubbed 'Influencers.' People with an Instagram or other social media account endorse a product or service which is provided to them free of charge and they get paid to say how good it is. If someone gives you something free and then pays you to comment about it, who do you think is ever going to say it's a piece of junk?

For these 'influencers' to have any traction with advertising clients they need to have between 10,000 – 50,000 followers. The more followers, the more they can charge their corporate clients. The average Instagram account holder has 150 followers so they can stay connected with their family and friends. The Kardashians are an influential family that has become famous – for being famous – and have made a lot of money in the process selling their own range of cosmetics, perfume and a variety of other fake procedures! This truly is an age of fake people, fake advertising, fake news, and, yes, fake relationships.

I was recently in a Melbourne courtroom waiting area, which is a great place to observe many aspects of society. I saw a young lady walk in who looked vaguely familiar. A quick glance revealed the obviously enhanced fake lips and it appeared to me, that she had purchased a range of other cosmetic enhancements. It seems she was trying to present herself in a way that nature had not given her naturally. The attempts made to 'enhance' her had not gone as well. It saddened me a little, because underneath it all there was a beautiful young lady. Her heavily tattooed male partner had also some work done and the way he walked seemed to mimic the gangsters portrayed in a movie about rappers living in the Broncs.

As I casually observed these two, it dawned on me that they were generic fake representations of the people I see flash past me when subscription and public television stations promote their growing stable of reality programs. Married at First Sight. Love at First Bite. Love Island, Blind Date, The Bachelor or Bachelorette. I had no idea which TV "stars" they were trying to emulate? They looked vaguely familiar – but obviously fake.

Fake news, fake looks, fake relationships, fake friends, fake likes, fake followers…fake, fake, fake. Do you think we have a problem here? In what ways do we think the fake world we live in spills over to subtly influence the approach we end up adopting as we develop our own relationships?

The solution is to *'Go About'*. Let's change direction. Let's truly value each other. Let's learn to connect with each other in meaningful ways. Let's value our friendships – at least the real ones. Let's be real in our workplace. Let's be more transparent and flee the fake stuff. Let's stop counting the number of "likes" and start counting the number of genuine engagements we have with others.

As you read this book, I have given you some tools to understand and learn how to move from merely making a connection with someone, to engaging with and fostering **real**ationships not for its own sake but in order to develop real life skills that can be used to change the world, a nation, or to influence family and communities.

Are you prepared to work with me and learn how to 'Go About'?

REFLECTION

Deciding to *Go About*: Why we need to change direction in our relationships.

Consider the following questions. Write down your answers, make notes in the margin of the chapter. Absorb what is helpful for you, jot down some questions. Pass on an idea to someone else.

1. In what areas do I need to *'Go About'* (change direction) in my life?

☐
☐
☐

2. What specific change is required to help me be more effective, efficient and engaging?

☐
☐
☐

3. In what way can I follow Bill and Melinda's example by "investing in the poor"?

☐
☐
☐

4. How absorbed am I in chasing fake news / friends / likes / relationships / looks? How does this affect my daily life?
- ☐
- ☐
- ☐
- ☐

5. What is the most difficult relationship(s) I have to manage?

_____

_____

6. What must I do to bring about significant change in my relationships?
- ☐
- ☐
- ☐

7. Personal Notes:

STEP 2

Discarding the cookie cutter: Treating everyone as *bespoke*.

> *"You can make more friends in two months by becoming interested in other people, than you can in two years by trying to get other people interested in you."*
>
> – DALE CARNEGIE

I am privileged to have led an amazing life. I've travelled the world and have visited over 80 countries. I have been to some countries 10, 15, or 20 times. I have spent 18 months on the African continent, at least a year on the Indian continent and cumulatively, years living in Asia and Europe.

I got married to my wife Julie in New Zealand in 1976. In 1978, we decided to move to Melbourne, where my brother and Julie's sister lived. The plan was to settle down, get a job, save some money and then travel to Europe to have a look around: do some backpacking, do what New Zealander's referred to as the "O.E." - the overseas experience.

Having got the O.E. out of our system, our plan was to settle back in Christchurch, New Zealand, and live what we thought at the time, was a 'normal' life.

Getting a job in Melbourne was not that difficult in the late 70's and the wages in Melbourne were about twice what they were in New Zealand. However, saving enough money and actually leaving to head off overseas became more of a challenge. We made friends and became part of a local church community, helping run the youth group. We even bought a house. In the winter we skied. In the summer we sailed. We were exactly what the advertising gurus referred to as D.I.N.K.S.- Double Income, No Kids. The marketers loved us, and we were the target of all the goodies that they wanted us to purchase with our hard-earned money.

In 1980 we heard about a little ship that was traveling around the world called the MV Logos. The purpose of the ship was to distribute educational literature to those that could not afford it or could not access good books in their own countries.

Volunteers operated the ship—and these volunteers actually paid a fee to be on the ship and travel the world. The MV Logos visited Melbourne, but we were too busy to go and see it. It was probably just as well. If we'd walked on board the MV Logos, we likely might have decided there was no way we could ever live on that little bathtub!

Some friends had visited the vessel and said it was a great setup, staffed by an amazing group of predominantly young people. Through a range of circumstances, we were encouraged to join the crew of the MV Logos, and in August 1981, Julie and I walked up the gangway of the ship, which at the time was berthed in the deep-water container terminal in Singapore.

REALationships

Walking across the dock we weaved our way around the 40-foot containers stacked five high and being moved around like Lego blocks. The straddle cranes, which themselves were five stories high, zipped around the port. As we approached the MV Logos, we realized just how tiny the little vessel was. The host assigned to us gave us a warm welcome and after a quick tour of the ship, took us downstairs and showed us our cabin. It was tiny. Three meters long and just over two meters wide. A hand basin, a drop-down double bed that was a couch during the day and the only connection with the outside world was a small round porthole 30 cm across.

When our host left we shut the door and breathed in deeply. I clearly remember Julie turning to me and asking, "How on earth are we going to survive in this tiny cabin for the next two years of our life?" Reality had hit us like a runaway straddle crane chasing a container.

*Real*ational capacity develops with life experience.

Only a few weeks later, we were in the port of Chittagong in Bangladesh. We had finished our evening meal and decided to go for a walk.

Strolling down the gangway we made our way through the port gates straight onto the streets of Chittagong. We were impacted by the families living alongside the road, cooking over open fires. Life was lived by these people right out on the street. People were jammed in side by side, almost on top of each other. There were no toilets- at least nothing that flushed! Open defecation was the norm. Naked kids were running through the maze of dirt roads and alleyways. They seemed happy and engaged. Skinny men, wearing only a loin cloth, strained as they pulled their old wooden rickshaws along the dirt road ladened down with their passengers and their shopping, on their way to deliver them to their homes.

After a couple of hours absorbing the sights, sounds and smells, we finally returned to our ship. We walked up the gangway, we were checked in by the watchman and then we made our way down the clean stairs to our little cabin. All we wanted to do was to have a shower and wash off the dirt and smell we feared had clung to us. We later learned that this is a classic sign of culture shock.

As we went downstairs to our cabin and I opened the door for Julie, she looked in at the cabin and then at me. "Richard" she said, "God has given us a palace to live in for the next two years!"

It wasn't our plan, but we spent the next six years of our lives living on board two different ships. We worked with 40 different nationalities, all volunteers, who came to help and to learn by serving in the galley, the engine room or on deck, maintaining the vessel and ensuring our safe passage. I was responsible for the distribution of our quality literature: we had books in English and in local languages. Locals could come aboard and buy books with their local currency. There was always a queue of thousands of people, every day, lining up to visit this unique ship.

Through it all, we learned what it meant to live in community. We got to forge some amazing friendships, some we still maintain today. We travelled the world, learned a lot about ourselves and did all we could to help those who couldn't help themselves. During these six years, I gained a depth of understanding about cultures, people and personalities both within our on-board community and the public who came to visit the ship and buy a book.

We engaged with a huge range of guests. Everyone was welcome onboard. The vessel was open to the public and visitors were a varied lot. Some were illiterate, poor and curious. Others were port and custom officials, and local and national dignitaries. Presidents, Prime Ministers and Lord Mayors came on-board for official receptions which we hosted in each port and in every nation we visited. They had heard about this strange little ship with its 140 volunteers and wanted to see for themselves this unique example of a 'floating United Nations.'

The difference, many observed was that WE were actually united!

The richness of this experience over six years gave us opportunities we could not have gained in any other way. Julie and I learned step by step how to meaningfully engage with people who looked at the world from their lens and saw it differently from the way we perceived it. The wonderful transformation that took place was that in the richness of this experience our worldview changed as well. We began to recognise the cultural nuances that often divide us and make us see 'others', as different. Language. Food. Societal values. Religion. Worldview.

There was clearly no possibility to apply a cookie cutter approach with people, because everyone, I learned, is an individual. We are all unique, we are all special. A cookie cutter is used in a kitchen or bakehouse and is made of plastic or metal. They are designed to cut shapes. The same shape, the same size, time after time after time.

People are made differently, even within the same culture. There is no cookie cutter that can stamp out the same personality with the same worldview and the same approach to life.

We are all different. We are all unique individuals. So, we must throw away the cookie cutter in all our relationships, and actually start treating people as unique, bespoke and special.

Each of us is an individual. We are given a personality, one that is moulded and shaped by the environment in which we live, the family in which we were raised, the jobs that we do, the education that we receive and the way that life has been modelled to us by significant others. From childhood, we learn how to relate to others by watching those who raised us - whether it was correct or not. We all come to our teenage years and then adulthood carrying baggage from our upbringing. Some of it is great and some of it is not so good.

I learned this lesson on my first visit to India. In 2020 there were 1.4 billion people in India. In the early 80's there were *only* 720 million. I fell into the trap of thinking that all Indians were the same. They live in the same country, have similar features, speak Hindi and all wobble their heads when they are talking to you. (My sincere apologies to all my Indian friends!)

I could not have been more wrong! With my life experience now and being in a **REAL**ationship with many Indians, I see India as a smorgasbord of language, culture, food, immense socio-economic diversity and a tapestry of rich cultural heritage. My initial 'cookie cutter' approach was just plain wrong, wrong, wrong!

I shared in the last chapter about the influence my mother had on me. I want to acknowledge that the way I live my life today was largely influenced by what I was taught and what I observed in my parents' lives. I wish that everyone had the opportunity for the same privileged upbringing and education that I received.

I actually believed that everyone else was just like me and had the same sort of family life I had. It didn't take long before I realized that I was one of the privileged ones. The old book says that to whom much is given, much is required. And it has been incumbent on my life to give a lot because throughout my life I have received so much. I am rich beyond measure.

I love doing what I do. And I have had, to date, an amazing life because of the fact that I stepped out and did things that were different to the way many others live.

So how does all this relate to **real**ationships?

Bespoke instead of cookie cutter

I want to apply the concept of bespoke, as we think about our relationships.

The word *bespoke* conjures up for the fashionistas, Saville Row, in London. It is a famous street where clients go to purchase beautiful handmade, handcrafted suits, cut perfectly to fit every shape and size. They are made with the finest cloth, procured from the finest manufacturers in the world and assembled by the most skilled tailors on the planet.

If we approach our relationships in the same bespoke way, it means that we recognise no two people are the same. We must treat each person individually. Our relationships must be handcrafted, carefully managed, and developed over time. They must be designed to suit the circumstance and nurtured wisely to protect, support and maximise mutual benefit.

If we try to treat everyone the same, it is a bit like buying a suit off the rack. We will end up with something that will "do the job." The fit will be compromised and the sleeves a bit short – but hey, it's still a suit! By treating everyone the same we automatically adopt a cookie cutter approach to our relationships. Some relationships may work, we will annoy a few people along the way - but we will get the job done. What we will never realise is the number of people we will disappoint and we will miss out on relationships with people, who would love to engage with us at a bespoke level.

By contrast, if we treat each individual as bespoke, we then intentionally customize our engagement with them. Our attitude, our approach, the questions we ask, how we connect with them must suit their personality and expectation. We must think *bespoke* when it comes to all of our **real**ationships. We need to treat our life partner differently to our business partner. We need to think about how to best manage our clients - to meet their felt-needs and requirements. We need to learn how to best communicate with our kids. A two-year-old needs to be addressed very differently compared to a teenager. When we think **real**ationships, we must think bespoke!

REALationships require capacity to listen...

Stephen Covey, in his book *Seven Habits of Highly Effective People*, said that we must *'seek first to understand before being understood.'* I can't recall all the other habits, but I have always remembered this one and endeavour to apply it in my own relationships.

Whenever I have a business meeting with a new or potential partner, I consciously try to spend 50 minutes of the hour focusing on them, trying to understand what it is that drives them and motivates them. I seek to establish what it is they are looking for. It is only when I have truly understood their needs that I can use the last 10 minutes of our conversation to tailor (bespoke) what I am able to offer into that relationship. What I then present and the way in which I do it are now based on the understanding of where they are coming from. This may possibly be the most effective 10 minutes of my entire day!

The majority of my time is spent as CEO of the Entrust Foundation. A small, private foundation that seeks to help the poorest people on the planet. We identify trusted partners living in very in difficult parts of the world. We focus on East African India and Asia. Me and my project managers visit these amazing people, get to know them, develop a trusted relationship with them. We undertake our due diligence on them and their organisations. We agree on what they will do, how it will be funded and what outcomes we are expecting. I am then able to offer these well thought through community development projects to those that are interested in funding them. Entrust has an investment fund which covers all our overhead costs. That way 100% of every donation is used to help provide education, water and sanitation, economic empowerment or is used to combat human trafficking.

Part of my role as CEO of Entrust is to develop partnerships with high net-worth friends, people who have set up their own fund or manage trusts and foundations. My role has developed into one of friend, confidant and sounding board for them. Very wealthy people have a surprisingly small number of people with whom they can have open conversations about money, wealth or philanthropy. It takes time to build trust. One friend tells me, "I am always happy to have lunch with you Richard, because I know you are not going to pressure me for a donation!" Interestingly, donors become friends and friends become donors.

If I was just to blurt out my spiel, I might realise afterwards that it is of no interest to them and is of little or no value to their business. I have then simply wasted both their time and mine.

Seeking first to understand before being understood is one of the most important lessons any of us can learn in any business or personal relationship.

In a business relationship, the connection is developed by being curious; a person feels welcomed, we connect, the opportunity becomes engaging, the solution is integrated into a deal or arrangement. This in turn becomes the makings of a **real**ationship.

It's impossible to be integrated with someone in business unless we are first curious about what we can do together. We can't be engaged with someone in a business sense unless we have a strong connection. We can't do any of the above unless we are in a relationship with them.

Relationships are complex. None are as simple as they appear. Those we will engage with are all at different stages in their own personal and business relationships. These levels of complexity often drive our reactions in business and at home. In our minds we struggle to know how to manage. We could be separated, divorced, widowed, broken-hearted, lonely or rebounding. We may be *'single and loving it'*, or perhaps only looking for *friends with benefits*? We may have moved in our personal relationship from "it's complicated" to dating, to committed and wondering if it too old fashioned to get engaged. Do we marry or move in together? What does the transition from newlywed to happily married look like? We may be in a same-sex relationship, unsure how to manage life's demands.

This simply serves to remind us that the relational spectrum is vast and complex, therefore we need to manage all our connections wisely. We can't run before we walk. We can't jump before we know how to crawl. If we truly wish to be relational in every friendship and connection that we have, then we must treat each one as bespoke.

We recognise that the levels of complexity come with the territory. We cannot isolate ourselves or treat everyone the same when we approach relationships individually. When we seek the best we can for the other person, when we seek first to understand before we are understood, then we have the beginnings of a solid foundation for a strong relationship.

REALationships are often vertical.

Life and relationships are complicated, and there are often edges that blur into each other. It's difficult to know how we can best manage them. We all know people who know the same people. We often hold information about them that is inappropriate to share with others who know them.

In order to manage the complexities of being in relationship with people who are connected closely to each other, I have learned to manage these by approaching them on an individual basis. Each relationship is kept within the boundaries of that connection. I do not cross the line and share confidences from one to another. I refer to these as vertical relationships.

It's a bit like a grain silo that I saw as I was driving the 800 kilometres from Melbourne to Adelaide recently for a friend's wedding. In the wheat belt of Victoria in Australia, they were harvesting grain. The grain was being stored in the huge silos and the silos were individually built, but they were connected to each other with a small auger. This makes it possible to take the grain from them.

This is a good example of how we should manage our relationships. We are connected at a basic level, but what is in each silo needs to remain within that silo. We do not share information between relationships that could compromise, or give information to others, that may not be appropriate.

If we are to be serious about managing our relationships, we need to learn how to run vertical relationships, in order to build trust and not to compromise the information that we have across our relational silos. The things we say about others will affect the complexity of our relationships. Managing vertical relationships and keeping information, personal and private as appropriate, will help build trust and will enable us to be effective across all the relationships that we manage.

Richard Beaumont

If you have a relationship cookie cutter, do everyone a favour and put it in the recycle bin. Understanding where people come from and where they sit on the relational spectrum will help us engage in a personal and meaningful way. In every relationship, we need to recognize that there are many levels of complexity. Let's not be naive about the words we use. Give some thought to our body language, how others perceive us and what our non-verbal communication is saying to them.

I have been the CEO of the Entrust Foundation for the last 12 years. I joined the board of our parent organization 20 years ago. During this time, I have had the privilege of building trusted ***real***ationships with some of the poorest people on the planet. I've also been able to build trusted ***real***ationships with some of the wealthiest.

My role is essentially one of a dot joiner. I know the needs in the developing world and have trusted relationships with the people we work with, to help meet those needs at a local level. I'm also connected with people of means who have the capacity to fund the projects that we identify.

One of life's secrets, I have learned, is to treat everyone in a bespoke way. For those of us working in the developing world, understanding their financial situation, the nation in which they live, the politics of that nation, the socio-economic challenges, their personal circumstances and their own life challenges. Because I have learned to treat everyone as bespoke, I am in a strategic position to help develop the relationships that the wealthy can have with the poor, that they are wanting to help.

It's only when we get these ducks in a row, that we can begin to assess the suitability of the local partner to manage the funds with which we will entrust them. Once we are there, we then need to find a donor who may have a passion to help these people. If my relationship is not strong and trustworthy and transparent, then there is little hope for any development that we fund, to become successful or effective.

REALationships

REALationships are open, honest and transparent.

At Entrust, we pay regular in-country visits to our partners. Most of them work in extremely difficult economic circumstances. The temptation for them is to tell foreigners what they think the foreigner wants to hear. We want to build a trusted relationship with our local partners where they can be transparent and where we can trust them to tell us exactly what is going on. Because we have high trust and low expectations in this unusual relationship, they are free to tell us the good, the bad, and the ugly. They do so because they trust us, and they trust the strength of the relationship.

It's only when we have open, transparent, honest communication with each other that we can begin to help each other and achieve a better outcome for everyone.

I was recently in a country in East Africa with my colleague, Jenny, the project manager for that nation. She told me that she thought there were some issues with an organisation we had been supporting, but she couldn't quite put her finger on it.

When we met our partners, we spent the first few minutes in the car traveling to the agriculture project and country area. As it was my first time to meet them, after we had said our greetings and got to know each other a little in the car on the way to the project site, I made a statement which shocked them:

"If you tell me that everything is going well, I will not believe another word that comes out of your mouth."

They were a bit taken aback and said, "What do you mean?"

I said, "I know that when funders come from overseas, you are tempted to tell us what you think we want to hear, so that you won't disappoint us, and so that we won't withdraw our funding."

I continued, as they stared open-mouthed, "We understand that, but we prefer open and transparent communication."

If they tell us that everything has gone well – (we know that rarely everything works out perfectly with development projects in challenging nations) - and they are not open with us about any concerns they have, we may have to review our funding.

"However," I added, "If you're willing to be open and transparent with us, and we can discuss the problems honestly and openly, we will work with you to help fix them. We will help, guide, and coach you so that you can be effective in what you are doing."

During the next 12 hours, they poured out their hearts to us and told us all the things that had gone wrong with their project and with the leadership of their organization.

It didn't surprise Jenny and me - her BS radar had already picked it up! We spent the day listening and asking questions. We then offered to meet with their Board the next day. Because of their transparency we were able to put in place some structure and some suggestions that made them strong and enabled us to continue funding them. Without that open approach the organisation would have died a slow and painful death.

This is just one of many examples I could share of open and honest communication, where there was a win-win for everyone involved.

No cookie cutter allowed here!

> *"In many ways, effective communication begins with mutual respect, communication that inspires, and encourages others to do their best."*
>
> – ZIG ZIGLAR

REFLECTION

Discarding the cookie cutter: Treating everyone as *bespoke*.

Consider the following questions. (Now or later on.) Write down your answers, make notes in the margin of the chapter. Absorb what is helpful for you, jot down some questions. Pass on an idea to someone else.

1. How do I use a cookie cutter approach in my relationships?

☐
☐
☐

2. What experiences have I been through that makes me who I am now?

☐
☐
☐
☐

3. In what ways have I been more prone to share my thoughts and plans without thinking of the other person's side?

☐
☐
☐

4. What specific changes can I make in the way I talk with others to help me be more intentional at listening and understanding them?

☐
☐
☐

5. Why do I tend to gloss things over instead of being honest and transparent? How can I combat these challenges and choose to be open and transparent?

☐
☐
☐
☐

6. Who are the people I find most difficult to understand?

_____

_____

7. What must I do to bring about significant change?

☐
☐
☐

8. Personal Notes:

STEP 3

Developing 'Selfie' awareness – how do others *really* see me?

> *"There she goes again, another selfie with the exact same facial expression, pose and head tilt. Just a different top this time. Nice, I can't wait for the next one."*
>
> - ANONYMOUS

We live in an obsessed world - one that is obsessed with… itself. However, you may be surprised to learn that the selfie trait is actually 181 years old! The first 'self-photo' was taken by Robert Cornelius in 1839. He had to stand still for 15 minutes to achieve the correct exposure. A far cry from the reality we have to contend with today! The hand-phone manufacturer Samsung recently did a survey about selfies and found that in the 18 – 24 age group, 30% of all photos taken were selfies.

Richard Beaumont

Driven even harder by Apple and a myriad of other phone designers and corporations, we now have forward-facing cameras, selfie sticks, remote controlled and self-timer camera phones, built with the express purpose of enabling us to indulge our need to show the world where we are, who we are and how beautiful we look. I have often wondered whether consumers drive designers or whether designers drive our consumer behaviour - helping manufacturers produce products that enable us to follow the latest trend!

It seems to me that selfies act as their own mirrors. We post them on Instagram, Snapchat, Facebook and a myriad of other apps, for our friends – and hopefully the media—to see. They reveal the perfect image we choose to present to the world at large: photoshopped, cropped, softened, and of course, with any imperfections removed. Selfies seemingly safeguard us against the fear of losing control of our image, our life as we wish to present it and possibly our minds!

Psychiatrists report that selfies appear to have evolved to become a natural instinct that will reduce our anxiety. But do selfies reduce our anxiety or instead, increase our stress levels? We only want people to see us the way we wish to present ourselves; edited images, in controlled, exciting environments where our lives are presented as awesome! We only ever hang out in fabulous locations, with large numbers of our chic friends who always look stunning and only own designer clothes. Not as we *really* are – when we are tired, grumpy, feeling depressed, going through the mundane chores of everyday life, or when we are having a 'bad hair day.'

But what does all this have to do with **real**ationships?

Self-awareness is not something you can photoshop, learn at university or purchase online. It is the art of understanding who we *really* are. We must learn to discipline ourselves and our busy lives. We have to stop long enough to consider who we genuinely are – to have a deep look into our own hearts.

The Covid-19 lock-down across the world in early 2020 gave us all the chance to reflect on the values that are important to us. A lot of what we took for granted was reviewed after it was removed from us – at least for a while. Things that we previously thought were ours by right, such as shopping, access to clubs, bars and restaurants, holidays, visiting our parents or our grand-children and the freedom to travel the globe. They were all removed from us in an instant! That made us re-think the aspects of our life that are privileged and helped us re-evaluate what is *really* important.

It is a healthy exercise to recognise our strengths - the areas in which we are gifted. It is even more advantageous to consider our weaknesses, the gaps in our lives where we need to develop. Simply acknowledging that we are not good at everything is a very healthy place to start in reaching our goals of self-awareness. I get a weekly video clip from British author Marcus Buckingham who has done extensive research into the team member appraisal process. He found that we will get further in life and business, and be more effective, when we focus on our strengths - not dwell or fret unnecessarily over our shortcomings. Whether we are making a personal assessment or conducting an appraisal for a person that is accountable to us, the same principle applies. Develop others' strengths and place far less emphasis on areas of weakness.

One of my Realational secrets is that I have been able to build into my hectic life and schedule a consistent time for reflection, meditation, reading, prayer and silence. I have made this a priority and have developed a quarterly cycle that seems to work for me. Every month I take time out for reflection, prayer and self-evaluation. Month one, I take a half day, month two a full day, month three two days, including an overnight stay away from home and any work-related activity. When I stop each month for this 'time out', I strive to go *off the grid* for the time allocated No phone, computer, text or TV. I am still learning to slow down and listen, because driven people, find this is really difficult. Stopping long enough to listen to my heart is fuel for the journey.

> *"Your visions will become clear only when you can look into your own heart. Who looks outside, dreams; who looks inside, awakes."*
>
> — C.G. JUNG

As Carl Jung suggests in this quote, when we look into our own heart, our true motivation, the goals, the gaps and flaws become apparent and we can start to deal with them. We learn what we previously did not know because we have taken the time to 'listen'. We don't know what we don't know, and this is one way to expose ourselves to the danger of knowing a little more about ourselves! I do not know what faith you may follow, if any. You may meditate, practice yoga, chant, pray, read philosophy, the Bible or the Koran. Whatever you do, this principle applies. We must STOP for long enough, on a regular basis, to examine our hearts and our lives, and only then will we be awake to the true motivation we have in all of our *real*ationships.

> *Self-awareness is our capacity to stand apart from ourselves and examine our thinking, our motives, our history, our scripts, our actions, and our habits and tendencies.*
>
> — STEPHEN COVEY

Learning to become self-aware will take time, effort, openness, honesty and maturity.

Let's work together and unpack this statement, to reveal what it is saying to us.

Stand apart from ourselves….

As Covey puts it, the concept of *"standing apart from ourselves"* is challenging. I have suggested that one way to do that is by making time for reflection. Another way we can begin to do this is within the safety net of a trusted **real**ationship. This appears to be a stumbling block in itself. How can I trust someone with my innermost secrets, while working on my self-awareness? Most people have what some describe as a *"Besty"*. A close friend, partner or caring individual with whom we can be completely open and honest. Perhaps I am more fortunate than most, because there are a number of people in my life with whom I am free to be completely open and transparent.

I have a personal mentor called John. We talk most months, depending on his schedule and mine. He is often tough on me and he asks the hard questions few others will ask. He is welcome to dig, probe, encourage and holds me accountable for the things I have committed to do, but haven't quite got to yet! He is sometimes clinical but cares for my personal well-being. He genuinely wants the best outcomes possible for me and subsequently the organisation I run. He shows concern for my family, my health, my spiritual vitality. He always asks a defining question whenever we connect: *"How much charge is in your emotional battery?"* I have to give John an answer between 1–10.

It is a great question because running our emotional battery down a very low ebb is like ignoring the low oil warning light on our car dashboard. If we ignore the warning light long enough, we hope it will simply go away and fix itself. If we continue driving without addressing the issue of no or low oil, the engine we will eventually seize the motor and destroy it. The only way to make it work once again is to undertake a complete re-build. This is a lesson that is applicable to each of us.

During one mentoring appointment at the end of a very full year my emotional battery got down to a '3.' It was mid-November, and John suggested I take a week's leave BEFORE Christmas! Laughing at him, I asked, "which Christmas?"

In spite of the mayhem that always evolves pre-Christmas, I was able to fit in a week off, and my emotional battery level lifted as I closed out the year. Without a mentor to push me, that would never have happened. I am so grateful that I have someone outside my immediate world who can see me for who I am and where I am at – and guide me towards what is best for my well-being and ultimately my organisation, my team and family too.

Several times a year, I travel overseas to provide concentrated input with Entrust's friends and partners in some of the poorest nations on earth. I have undertaken well over 50 of these trips since starting Entrust in 2008! I regularly return home exhausted with a very low emotional charge in my personal battery. I have expended a lot of physical and emotional energy to engage in a meaningful way – in **real**ationship with those living in dire circumstances.

This is not just a *job* for me. It is a lifetime commitment to do all I can to bring hope in some of the hardest places on earth. I do not consider myself a hero in any way. I do this to utilise the realational skills that have been modelled to me - and which I have been able to fine-tune, in order to make the biggest impact I am capable of in the lives of some of the poorest people on the planet.

As we continue to look at Covey's quote about self-awareness, we need to review some of the key elements of our life.

REALationships

Examine our...

1. Thinking.
   - ☐ What do I dwell on?
   - ☐ Am I looking for the best for others - or only what I can get out of it?
   - ☐ What shapes the way I think?
   - ☐ What do I read and watch?
   - ☐ What external influences capture my thoughts?

2. Motives.
   - ☐ Do I have a hidden agenda?
   - ☐ Am I greedy or generous?
   - ☐ Will I take 'short cuts' to get what I want?
   - ☐ What is my life goal? Do I even have one?

3. History.
   - ☐ Have I dealt with my past?
   - ☐ Have I thanked my parents for the upbringing they gave me?
   - ☐ Have I forgiven them if I have been disappointed and feel they let me down?
   - ☐ Am I holding a grudge that is holding me back?
   - ☐ What lessons have I learned from my past mistakes and successes?
   - ☐ Do I consider my history in order to guide and direct my future journey?

4. Scripts.
   - ☐ Do I believe what others say? (Good and bad).
   - ☐ Have I been told I will come to nothing?
   - ☐ Have I been told, "You can do anything"?
   - ☐ Have I fallen for the mantra 'You are awesome'!
   - ☐ What 'script' do I follow – is it wise?

5. Actions.
   - ☐ Do I talk or do?
   - ☐ Do I deliver what I say?
   - ☐ Do I turn up on time – every time?
   - ☐ Do I leave everything until the last minute?
   - ☐ Do I plan ahead and use my time well?

- ☐ Do I engage in helping others in need?
- ☐ Do I give my money / time generously and with joy?

6 Habits.

- ☐ What are the things I am addicted to?
- ☐ Can I name 6 good habits?
- ☐ Can I identify 3 bad ones?
- ☐ How will I work on my bad habits?
- ☐ Do my habits define me?
- ☐ Are my habits an excuse for not taking responsibility?

7. Tendencies.

- ☐ Do I tend to exaggerate?
- ☐ Do I tend to procrastinate?
- ☐ Do I tend to lie?
- ☐ Do I tend to put others down?
- ☐ Do I tend to complain?
- ☐ Do I tend to make excuses?
- ☐ What do I tend to do? _____ (fill in your response)

As we work through the list, (now, or during your reflection time) write down a specific answer to each of the points. Writing it down forces us to articulate what it is we are dealing with. Keep a diary or journal of what we observe, refer back to the notes and observations we have made, or lessons recorded - and hopefully learned. This discipline has been significant in helping me to become more self-aware.

Charles Sykes is a journalist and the host of a radio talk show in Milwaukee USA and a senior research fellow at the Wisconsin Policy Research Institute. He has written for newspapers including The New York Times, The Wall Street Journal, and USA Today. He is the author of several books, including, 'Dumbing Down Our Kids'. (2).

REALationships

Sykes sets out 11 rules of life in his book. You may have already read these rules – they have been floating around the internet for 20 years. Often wrongly attributed to Bill Gates, you could be forgiven for stating they are obviously written by a 'baby boomer.' In all seriousness, there is a lot of truth in these statements and if you are serious about becoming more self-aware, take some time to look through the list with an open mind and see what insights you may learn about yourself.

Here are the 11 rules.

1. "Life is not fair – get used to it." The more time you spend complaining about the things you can't control, the less time you'll devote to the things you can.

2. "The world doesn't care about your self-esteem." Respect is earned, not given. You need to achieve something on your own, in order for others to stand up and applaud your contribution.

3. "You won't earn $80,000 right out of high school." You'll need to work your way up, and – in many ways – the lessons and failures you experience along the way will serve as your real education.

4. "If you think your teacher is tough, wait till you get a boss." In many cases, it's your tuition that's paying the teacher. In the business world, it's the teacher who's paying you.

5. "Flipping burgers is not beneath your dignity." When your grandparents were young, flipping burgers was an opportunity to learn.

6. "If you mess up, it's not your parents' fault… It's yours." Don't waste time blaming others. They'll resent you, and it doesn't earn you any real respect.

7. "Take responsibility for your own contribution, rather than waiting for others to place opportunities in front of you." Don't waste years of your life waiting for someone to show up on your doorstep and hand you the roadmap to success. Go out and grab it.

8. "Your school may have done away with winners and losers, but life has not." Hard work is often its own reward. And consistent hard work leads to greater rewards.

9. "Life is not divided into semesters and you won't have the summers off." Make time for yourself but devote yourself to being focused and equal to the task on a daily basis.

10. "Television is not real life." You need to step outside your comfort zone to really experience life.

11. "Be nice to nerds … Chances are, you'll end up working for one."

Managing our reputation.
In this chapter we have discerned how we see ourselves and learned ways we can identify our own strengths, flaws and weaknesses. I want to close this chapter by thinking about what others say about us when we are *not* there. This is the worst nightmare possible for some people! The tendency is to want to control the conversation: the image we present is how we want others to see us (back to the selfie concept).

At Christmas time we all receive greetings and emails from friends, clients and family members wishing us a "Happy Christmas and a Wonderful New Year." They are well-meaning, I am sure, but the cynic in me says they are doing it out of societal obligation. As we approached the new decade 2020, I was touched by a good friend and Entrust partner 'RC' in India who wrote me a personal email in December.

REALationships

> *"Thank you very much for all your hard work and your sacrifice and partnership with God's work in India and other parts of developing world. We are so thankful for it. We hope to see you in India in the near future."*
>
> RC

It was accompanied by a family photo with his beautiful wife and two amazing daughters. It touched me and was such an encouragement because I knew it came straight from his heart. This is how RC sees me when I am not there. It is not about business or even community development, it is based on a **REAL**ationship.

RC and Entrust work together in central India combatting child sex trafficking and funding two informal schools – one in a shocking slum and the other in a snake charmers' village. When I visited with my colleague Kate, we feel loved and appreciated by our friend RC and his family's generous hospitality but also by the school teachers, the rescued girls and the snake charmers! Why they insist on putting a python around our necks is something I'm always unsure about, but enthusiastically embrace. We do this as much for the photos they take but more importantly for the way that this simple act helps us to connect and engage with their community. Everyone thinks it's hilarious and a bit of feigned horror on my part adds to the mood, fun and frivolity.

Any team member working with Entrust never allows ourselves to be the *'precious foreigner.'* I am always prepared to play the fool and make myself a little vulnerable. In doing so, I place myself alongside these gentle local people, build some rapport and in a small way seek to identify with their culture and their circumstance.

What do people say about you when you are not there? Does it worry you? Do you present yourself in different ways to different friends or clients?

Richard Beaumont

Not smart enough to lie!

Years ago, I worked out that I am not smart enough to lie. I would never be able to remember to whom I told which story. The reason I do not care what others say when I am not there is that I am Richard Beaumont – in every circumstance. I am not trying to be someone I am not. I seek to be open and honest in every **real**ationship because I am not smart enough to do it any other way!

Yes, there are varying levels of relationships and there are necessary boundaries – depending on who, what, where and when. I treat confidentialities very carefully; I try very hard not to gossip about others. I don't always meet my own very high expectations but I do my best to manage vertical relationships and endeavour to be transparent in all my dealings.

If you tell lies in any of your relationships I hope you have a photographic memory! You will spend a lot of emotional energy trying to juggle which story you told to whom. You will get caught out and when you do, your credibility, reliability and trustworthiness will be permanently tarnished and you will impose a limit on your own career. It is just not worth it!

Next time you take a selfie, be mindful of what it is you are trying to achieve. When we focus on the outside we are dreaming. When we look inside, we awake!

REFLECTION

Developing 'Selfie' awareness – how do others *really* see me?

Consider the following questions (now or later).

Write down your answers, make notes in the margin of the chapter. Absorb what is helpful for you, jot down some questions. Pass on an idea to someone else.

1. In what ways do I *'manufacture'* the perception I want others to have of me?

☐
☐

2. What is my *real* motivation for why and how I post selfies?

☐
☐
☐

3. Write down a description of the public image I would like to present – to everyone with whom I engage.

4. Of the "11 Rules" which is the *one* that challenges me the most?

☐ Rule # ____ because ...

5. This is the person/ people I will write an email to in the next 24 hours, to express my appreciation for what they mean to me / have done for me:

_____
_____

6. Other reflections / observations:

STEP 4

Don't touch that! – Five *real*ational 'No-Nos'

In sailing jargon, we often have to do a manoeuvre called a jibe. This occurs when you turn the back (stern) of the boat through the eye of the wind and the sail moves from one side of the boat to the other.

There are two types of gybes: a controlled jibe and an uncontrolled jibe. (You want to avoid the second one at all costs!) When the skipper plans a controlled jibe, it is a simple, planned manoeuvre and a good skipper will always warn his crew of a coming jibe by calling out "prepare to jibe!" For seasoned sailors, this is code for 'watch the boom' – the long metal beam that holds the bottom of the sail to the mast.

However, in conditions when the wind is gusting hard and constantly changing direction and if the skipper is distracted or not concentrating on the task at hand, an uncontrolled gybe can take place and surprise the skipper and crew in a heartbeat. This can be very dangerous as the sail and the attached aluminium boom, without warning, decides to move from one side of the boat to the other with great force and speed! The boom and sail will take out anything in its path including bodies, heads, hats, gear and whatever the boom hits on the way through. In these circumstances the boom travels at the same speed as the wind. At 50 kph I will leave it to you to work out what can go wrong and the damage and pain an uncontrolled jibe can cause!

Managing our relationships is just like jibing. When we are in control and know what is going on, life is simple and straightforward; we are composed and confident.

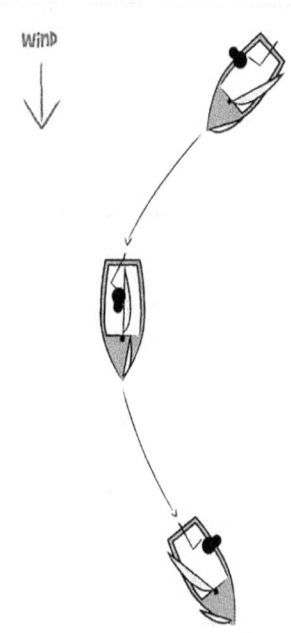

Sadly, that's not always the case. We have all found ourselves, at some point in our relational world, in the middle of an uncontrolled jibe. The wind shifted, we missed the indicators, we took our eye off the conditions, we failed to read the situation and we found ourselves in the middle of a storm. Our 'boom and sail' have changed sides without warning. It has hit us like an out-of-control tank, wrecked our plans, taken out a few of our people and caused some devastation in the process.

We now have to pick ourselves up, start to clean up, recognise the storm will pass and the wind will drop - eventually. We limp back to our berth, nursing our bruised ego, making sure our crew is OK, tending to our cuts and bruises vowing never to be caught in an uncontrolled, relational jibe again—ever!

Yes, we can convince ourselves that we learn so much through mistakes. But do we? There are a number of relational blunders we can avoid by simply understanding the damage they can cause. I have identified five relational 'No-No's' – blunders, stuff-ups, mistakes – call them what you will. There are many more than just these five, but when avoided, they will vastly improve our capacity to turn many relationships into REALationships.

Five *real*ational No-Nos:

1. Not listening.

> *"Most of the successful people I've known are the ones who do more listening than talking."*
>
> - BERNARD BARUCH

No one ever had to teach me how NOT to listen. How often have you been trying to concentrate on a task, and a friend, partner or colleague chooses that particular moment to start talking to you? If I have decided the task at hand is more important to me than the conversation they wish to start, I know I have all been guilty of responding with an, "Uh-huh," "Yep," "Sure," "OK," "Really?" - when I was not actually listening at all! We have no idea what we just acknowledged—a dangerous position in which to find yourself. But then I am sure *you* would never do that!

I work in an open-plan office and our busiest day each week is a Wednesday. This is the day I endeavour to get my whole team into the office. It is the day we connect, communicate, set up meetings, plan, prepare and report. It is difficult for all of us to get our key tasks accomplished, as we each grab the opportunity to connect.

Occasionally someone wants a quick answer to a question and pops their head over the dividers and starts talking across the office to a colleague who is sitting two desks away! In the meantime, the rest of us concentrating on work tasks at our computers are distracted -and sometimes frustrated! (The Entrust Foundation team are still endeavouring to build a protocol that maximises communication and minimises interruptions.)

Sarah is our very capable Operations Manager. She is a young mum with a long "to do" list – both at work and at home. I love working with her and we share a similar work style. Both of us have a good eye for what works, what's realistic and for getting stuff done. On a recent Wednesday she wanted my attention. Our desks are not too far apart and I was plugging away trying to reduce the volume of unread emails in my inbox. Suddenly I was aware of a loud whisper, *"BEAUMONT!!"*

I turned around and Sarah had a big grin on her face. I must have looked a little surprised as she had never called me by my surname in the two years we have worked together. She said, "I tried Richard, Richie, Richie Rich – all were ignored. I now have your attention!" I simply hadn't heard her, I wasn't listening, I was tuned out. It was a fun incident and we managed to destroy the entire team's concentration - for a moment. We all had a good laugh, then got back to work.

Listening is a critical aspect of a REALationship. NOT listening is a sure-fire way to be shut out, shut down or shut up. When we are really listening, we are giving our **real**ationship - at any level you care to name - every chance of success. Listening is a skill like any other; it has to be learned, refined and fine-tuned. It has often been said that we have been given two ears and one mouth. We must learn to use them in that proportion. In other words – do twice as much listening as talking.

How can we be better listeners? I have identified *six basic concepts,* which, when applied, will make us better listeners. You may already be aware of them or have read them somewhere. Making these principles a part of our day-to-day lives, applying and actually implementing them, is a matter of intentionality and practice.

Six ways to be a better listener.

1. *Make eye contact.* There is nothing worse than trying to have a conversation with someone who is looking at their shoes or looking over your shoulder. Look them in the eye, but don't stare them down – that can be intimidating for some! Be attentive to what they are saying. Sometimes repeating their words in your mind is a good way to concentrate on the message they are seeking to convey to you.

2. *Be open to what is being said.* Listen, understand, engage. Do not fall into the trap of hearing the first couple of sentences and then stopping your listening, while you formulate in your head the response you will offer to their words. An aid to better listening is to visualise in pictures what the person is seeking to convey. Keep an open mind, endeavour to understand their point of view – even if yours is different. Put yourself in their shoes and try to understand the point they are making from their perspective of the problem or issue.

3. *Do not interrupt* anyone while they are speaking. Even worse is to offer a solution before they have had the chance to explain the issue or problem! When we interrupt, several things happen simultaneously. The speaker feels unheard, they lose their train of thought and it is often difficult to capture their heart-cry after your interruption. By interrupting, we give them the impression that what *we* have to say is more important than what they were *trying* to communicate. This does not mean you can't acknowledge what they are saying. A nod, a smile, or a "that's right" affirms they are being heard and these communication cues will lift the engagement level for both parties. Simply put, interrupting when someone is talking breaks down communication, connection and engagement for us – and the other party as well.

4. *Mirror what the speaker is saying.* Chris Voss, an acclaimed international FBI hostage negotiator has written an excellent book titled "Never Split the Difference".[3] In his book, Chris describes a number of negotiating techniques including *mirroring*. You do this by repeating the last critical few words that have just been spoken. This demonstrates to the speaker you are empathising with them; you are in accord with them and that you are endeavouring to hear what they are seeking to communicate. The intention behind most *'mirrors'* should be *"please help me understand."*

A good example of this could be a conversation between a teenager and her parent. It is Friday night and as the daughter is about to head out the door she yells to her father, "Dad, I'm off, not sure when I will be home."

Dad mirrors, "Not sure?"

"Depends where we end up, could be a club or bar, and a group of us may go to my friend's holiday house overnight."

"Staying overnight?"

"I probably should have asked if it was OK with you and Mum to stay overnight," she responds.

"Is it OK?" her concerned father replies and waits.

The daughter thinks for a minute and says, "We did agree I would check with you before being out past midnight."

"Is this checking?" asks her Dad.

"I know you want me to be safe, Dad. Tell you what - I'll be home by midnight as we agreed."

Of course, this is a hypothetical conversation – and parents of teenage daughters may be asking, how many teenage daughters have you raised, Richard? But do you see how mirroring is non-confrontational and draws the speaker out? If the daughter had left home that Friday evening without having had the conversation, the parents may have next seen their daughter on Saturday evening after investing a very anxious 24 hours trying to call her mobile which now has a flat battery and track her down to ensure she is safe. Mirroring enables us to *hear* what the other is saying and *draw out* more information than was previously intended to be shared.

5. Seek to clarify the message. This is taking mirroring a step further by articulating in summary form, what the other person is saying. I have been the Chair of several organisations and in key leadership positions for over 35 years. I work best within a consensus style of leadership, so when there has been a complex discussion, with many voices and opinions and lots of options - all of them good - I believe it is the Chair's job to summarise what has been said and suggest a way forward, with which everyone can agree.

It may sound something like this: "It seems to me we have agreed that the change in government reporting requirements means we have to improve our documentation and more closely manage funds we are sending to our overseas partners. There have been several and varying opinions around the table, from engaging a law firm to advise us, to employing an extra person to manage this - neither of which are in our budget for this year. I propose that we consider adding extra compliance costs in next year's budget, and in the meantime, we appoint a Board/Staff working group to identify the areas that will affect us, in order to keep up with compliance requirements and establish what we need. Do we agree?"

When we clarify any message, we are giving feedback that results in one of two outcomes. Firstly, it confirms we understand what has been said and that we are in agreement. Secondly it gives the speaker the chance to say, "Actually that's not what I meant. I didn't suggest we *engage* a law firm, my friend is an outstanding lawyer who has room in his pro-bono budget for an organisation like ours and I would be happy to ask him to help us." This clarification serves to change the outcome and keep us all on the same page.

6. Label the unspoken fears. When we are empathetic, when we demonstrate the ability to understand and share the feelings of another, it doesn't require us to agree with them. Empathy does not put us in a position of compromise – it simply conveys we are listening. The reasons one *shouldn't* go ahead with a business deal or agreement are more powerful than why they *should*. By labelling unspoken fears it puts the negative emotions in the open, on the table for all to see. In many ways, having the concerns in plain sight makes it easier to deal with them because everyone now recognises the downside and what could go wrong.

I am a small-time investor, managing our small retirement fund. I am also part of a committee that makes investment decisions about the millions of dollars of capital we manage for the Entrust Foundation. Income generated from this fund pays for all the overhead costs of the organisation, in order to get 100% of our donor's funds to the project in the village on the other side of the world. A compelling model!

REALationships

Due to my engagement on our Investment Committee, I have learned to think like a professional investor and members of the committee have taught me how to understand risk. How? Because one of our Board Members, Matthew, is a highly skilled risk analyst and fund manager for both a major consulting business and a private equity firm. I often argue with Matthew that he is too conservative. His response is to simply refer me to our balance sheet and point out the growth he and the committee has helped us sustain over several years. He has helped us de-risk our portfolio in the current uncertain international climate. Matthew is one of my many mentors, for whom I am deeply grateful. The proof of this advice is that when the international money markets took a huge dive due to Covid-19 many investors lost 30% - 40% of their capital. We dropped 2%! Our advisors understood how to minimise risk.

One of the ways to assess an investment is not only to look at the returns it will bring - the upside - but to look long and hard at what could possibly go wrong. I am a *glass half-full* person. It would not be unfair to describe Matthew as a *glass half-empty* person. Over the years, Matthew has demonstrated his capacity to voice his concern in vivid images and to articulate what could go wrong. "Trump could sneeze and the world could catch pneumonia." "The Chinese/Hong Kong riots in late 2019 could cause chaos in the markets." "The 2020 Australian bushfires will negatively impact our economy." Sometimes I get to the point of feeling it may just be easier to hide the money under the mattress. If I did suggest this solution (and I haven't yet) Matthew would then *label* my fears by pointing out the possibility of a house fire, burglary or termite invasion!

Denying or ignoring barriers gives them credibility. When we label unspoken fears, it clears the barriers and helps us reach an agreement – one that is measured and well thought through. Next time you are making a presentation, state some of the negatives along with the opportunities being offered. Remember, you won't be saying anything that has not already been thought of. Instead, you will be putting them in the open in order to develop a deeper sense of well-being and increasing trust. Try it!

Our first relational 'No-No' is not listening.

> *"He who mistrusts should be trusted least."*
> – GREEK PROVERB

2. Insincerity.

> *"Sincerity is the key to success. Once you can fake that, you've got it made!"*
> - GROUCHO MARX

"Something is not right, and I can't quite put my finger on it," said Jenny, one of our Entrust project managers. "He says and does all the right things – just a little bit too well. There is something insincere about him that bothers me."

A few months later we were visiting this project together and had since found out that a small amount of the project's funds had not been used for what it was intended. We had been emailed copies of the official receipts to "prove" the money had been spent on what was in the budget. This was a small part of a bigger project in a very poor part of Africa. When we arrived, the right words flowed from our local partner but the excitement that had been generated, quickly disappeared when Jenny and I asked to see the textbooks that were *supposed* to have been purchased.

REALationships

Instead of admitting his failure and deception, our partner kept talking faster and faster, changing his story and seeking to assure us there had been a slight 'change of plan' but that it was all good. We offered multiple opportunities for this person to tell us what really happened and we would have worked out a way forward, with the hope that a mistake made and resolved, would have resulted in a stronger trust and deeper partnership.

Sadly, in this case (fortunately we have only had to deal with very few) the insincerity, obvious dishonesty and complete lack of transparency brought us to the point of having to conclude the relationship. It had deteriorated to the point where it fell well short of a REALationship.

Insincerity is a REALationship killer. You may think you are coming across well and all is good. Anyone with even half a casual look can see the insincerity a mile away! After 15 years in the philanthropic world working across multiple cultural settings, I think I have a pretty good - what I refer to as my "B.S. Radar." My colleague Jenny also has an outstanding radar. The combination of the two of us working together simply means – look out! You won't get much past us.

There are multiple ways to spot a fraud. Insincerity is one of the first *alerts* that will register on my B.S. Radar. If I am insincere, I pretend to be something I am not or present a situation in a way that I know to be untrue. Insincerity is on the continuum between something as subtle as an exaggeration to deliberately telling an outright lie. (We deal with lying next.) Insincerity is actually saying something you would *like* to be true whilst not believing it yourself. This presents to us an internal 'conflict of interest,' and we have all been guilty of insincerity.

I have learnt over many years that openness and transparency are far more effective tools to build trust, **real**ationship and positive outcomes in every circumstance. I have had many conversations with potential donor partners that go something like this:

"I am so pleased you are interested in partnering with Entrust. There are some things I need to alert you to when working with us – just so we are clear. It may cost more to do this than the budgeted amount. It may end up taking longer than we planned – and the end result may be different from what we expected! If you can live with this level of ambiguity, I am confident we can partner together and make the world a much better place. I sincerely believe that together, we can develop a valuable *real*ationship."

People then look at me somewhat incredulously and I just smile. This is usually followed by a comment like, "You're serious, aren't you!"

The reality is that 97% of our projects are very successful. Some don't go as planned, some take longer and sometimes cost more than we expect. In a somewhat light-hearted way, I find that by being up-front with people, even potentially scaring some off, I am able to better connect with those who are more realistic in their expectations. **Real**ationships are about pairing with like-minded people to mutual benefit. Community development is a risky endeavour. But then so is business.

Have you ever put together a business plan where your timelines, budgeted expenses and income projections happened exactly as planned? My guess would be, never! Establishing a new business from scratch is a deeply challenging task in a *developed* country where everything is stable. How would you go setting up your business in an *undeveloped* country where there could be a coup d'état next week, inflation running at 300%, where the supply chain is unreliable and where the government may withdraw large denomination notes from circulation, leaving you with worthless paper? Each of these events has taken place in some of the countries in which we work. Being realistic is a great start to any *real*ationship.

Sincerity is being honest, open, transparent and above board in every aspect of our conversation promises, emails, talk of others, agendas, goals and aspirations. Insincerity is none of these and will be a sure-fire way to destroy any chance of business or relational success. Insincerity is a *real*ational blunder to be avoided – at all costs!

3. Lying.

> *"True freedom is where an individual's thoughts and actions are in alignment with that which is true, correct, and of honour – no matter the personal price."*
>
> - BRYANT H. MCGILL

I mentioned earlier that I am not smart enough to lie. It is too difficult for me to remember to whom I told which version of the story! If we are to have any chance of a *real*ationship in business, friendship, marriage, socially – even in casual conversation - we must decide once and for all that lying is NEVER going to be an option for us! It is important to remember that we don't ever have to compromise our integrity to achieve our goals.

What happens when we lie or even exaggerate? We are ultimately setting ourselves up for future failure. Someone, somewhere, will find us out. Others will find out via a third party that something we told them was not accurate, was exaggerated or simply not true. Do you know someone who is a liar? How did you come to that conclusion? By finding out that what they said was not an accurate representation of the truth. In your mind you have labelled them a liar and this has resulted in you questioning everything they say. It undermines that individual's credibility - even when they are telling the truth!

Bryant H. McGill is a human potential thought leader, international bestselling author, activist, social entrepreneur and UN Global Champion. In his quote thought and action, (I used at the beginning of this section,) he reminds us of the principle of alignment. Our thoughts and actions must be *aligned* with what is true, correct and honourable. King Solomon - thought to be the wisest person ever to have lived, wrote about integrity over 2,000 years ago. It is recorded in the Bible where he states, "Whoever walks in integrity walks securely, but whoever takes crooked paths will be found out. (Proverbs 10:9)"

Do we wish to walk securely, or do we want to spend our lives hoping we don't get *'found out?'* Often, there is a personal price to pay for this level of integrity. When I am travelling through difficult borders in some tough countries, I am often asked for a bribe. To be fair I am possibly seen by the locals as a rich westerner who has come to exploit their nation and make a big fat profit, at *their* expense. (They mistake me for a businessman – even though I never wear a suit!)

In 2015 I was in Africa, trying to depart a regional airport in one of the most difficult nations to which I have ever been. Corruption was the worst I have ever experienced and I decided to count the number of times I was asked for a bribe – just to fly to my next in-country location. I had a ticket, yellow fever card passport and all my documents were in order. Between arriving at the airport's unsealed car park, until the time I actually stepped into the very tired departing aircraft, I was asked for a bribe twenty times!

In this nation, foreign visitors are required to go through an internal 'immigration check' at every point of arrival and departure. Boat, car or air, it doesn't matter. At one point during my departure process I was escorted by an immigration official – along with my local partner and a translator to meet the head of immigration in this regional backwater. We walked into a huge office, resplendent with a picture of the president on a wall behind his desk. He pointed to the other three who were accompanying me and with a flick of his hand, beckoned them out.

Here we were, just him and me. Seated behind a huge desk, he had three gold stripes on the epaulets of his neatly pressed uniform. He took my passport and yellow fever card and in excellent English asked, "What do you have for me, my man?"

I work on the principle of not paying for something for which I cannot get an official receipt - not to be arrogant, but to seek to demonstrate integrity. "I have my yellow fever card and passport, Sir," I replied smiling and looking him in the eye.

"No, no, you misunderstand me," he said, "What do you have for *me?*"

I smiled again and looked at him and said, "I have my travel papers, Sir."

"I see you have a business visa. Tell me about your business," was his next response.

After explaining that I was there to assist an agricultural project helping local farmers, he made a statement that I will never forget. "Ahhh, so you are here to help us, not to take from us?"

"Exactly, Sir," was my response. "It has been a privilege for me to come here and help your people grow better crops so they can feed their families. There is so much more that needs to be done, we are doing all we can to help."

With that statement, he opened my passport, stamped, stood up and put out his hand to shake mine. "Thank you for coming to our province, have a safe flight and come and see me next time you are here!" I was cleared to depart and took my seat in the aircraft. As I sat down, I reflected on what had just happened. I told the truth I made a friend. I did not take the easy path and slip him $20. And I felt satisfied. As the aircraft taxied toward the runway it slowly dawned on me that in one hour, in the next city I was visiting, I would have to do it all over again!

The easier path may have been to tell a lie and slip him some cash to speed up the process. I would have achieved the same result but not had the opportunity to build trust, make a new friend and demonstrate to him that not all Westerners are liars who are out to fleece them.

> *"A lie gets halfway around the world before the truth has a chance to get its pants on."*
>
> - SIR WINSTON CHURCHILL

4. Self-centredness.

> *"Pride gets no pleasure out of having something, only out of having more of it than the next man...*
> *It is the comparison that makes you proud: the pleasure of being above the rest. Once the element of competition is gone, pride is gone."*
>
> - C.S. LEWIS

The fourth relational blunder to be avoided – at all costs - is thinking that you are better than you are or better than the people you are engaged with. If we even begin to think this way, it will undoubtedly result in us becoming proud and self-centred. We will seek to direct all traffic, all attention towards ourselves. We will manipulate conversations to make ourselves the centre of attention, the life of the party, the person everyone wants to be with. The way self-centred people come across to others is often as a proud know-it-all. They are painful, selfish, boorish, tactless, ungracious, intolerant, discourteous and most of the time - just plain rude! The trouble is, if that's us - we don't even know it!

Charger or Drainer?

Another way to check as to whether we are self-centred is to ask the question, "Am I a *charger* or a *drainer*?"

I have a twin cylinder 650cc cruiser, bad-boy motorcycle. It didn't cost a fortune and I love riding it. It's big, it's black and chrome - and LOUD! You can hear me coming from two blocks away. I refer to it as my "Hardly-a-Davidson" because it is <u>not</u> a Harley, just a look-a-like. For fun, my niece Melanie, helped me make some decals that look like the Harley Davidson logo but actually say "Hardly-a-Davidson." It is my way of being a non-conformist and giving those that are paying attention a good laugh!

If I do not ride my motorcycle over winter the battery goes flat and I have to charge the battery in order to start the bike. Strangely, the charger looks a bit like the battery. Both are of similar size and colour. One charges, the other drains. Relationships, on the surface, all appear to be the same. Some relationships charge us, and others are a drain.

The battery will drain because it is having the life sucked out of it, to the point where it has nothing to give back. Relationships function in a similar way. REALationships are always two-way. They have the capacity to both give and take.

'Charging' something *gives* life, a drainer sucks the life *out* of it. Humans are just like this too. Some of the people with whom we engage give us life and charge our batteries. We love being with them, we do activities together. If they are a work colleague we will engage socially outside of work. 'Chargers' in a **real**ationship are like taking my motorbike for a ride through the hills on a hot sunny Sunday – it charges my battery.

On the other hand, there are people we all know who can only be described as complete 'drainers'. They suck the life out of us and give nothing back in return. They are often totally self-centred, single-minded and have very low EQ (Emotional Quotient or Intelligence). Not surprisingly, *drainers* often lack self-awareness and the ability to accurately recognise emotional cues, personal strengths and the limitations of others. Drainers fail to understand the actions of others and they do not know how to *give* in a relationship.

We all tend to shy away from people like this. Someone with a vibrant personality who is constantly self-centred will be tolerated but eventually pushed to the edge of any social group or gathering. In a business setting it becomes apparent that the person eventually believes *they* are more important than the task. Many *drainers* have no idea how they present to others. This makes it hard to work with them, difficult to manage them and tough to employ them. It inevitably puts up barriers to bosses, clients and colleagues. Being self-centred works actively *against* the very goals you may wish to achieve.

Years ago, my wife Julie and I had a friendship that we developed over several years. The friendship was not really for our benefit. Throughout our lives we have always tried to encourage those who find themselves on the fringes and our goal is to support them through life in whatever way we can, limited by our own time, emotional energy and capacity. Raymond (not his real name) would be invited to our home for meals several times a year. We would chat about his work, relationships, well-being, and faith and we would try to include him in social settings. He had some very strong opinions on many issues and tried to manipulate us into embracing his narrow and often bigoted viewpoint.

This friendship came to a grinding halt when, after inviting him to my birthday party at our home, he then asked if a certain guest would be attending. When I reminded Raymond that the guest in question was also a friend of mine and yes, he would be coming, he proceeded to berate me for inviting him when we knew that he and the other guest had opposing points of view! It was at this point Raymond had crossed a line. I suggested he was no longer welcome and that it was not his role to tell me who I could or could not invite to my own birthday party! This was no longer a relationship, let alone a **real**ationship. It could only be described as a one-way *drainer* - and to be honest, Julie and I both felt a sense of relief when the connection came to an abrupt end.

I am sure everyone reading this book could tell many stories similar to the one above. The challenge is knowing how and when to conclude a *drainer* relationship, so we can get on with the rest of our lives and invest in people that will *charge* us, taking great care along the way, to ensure that we are also a *charger*. We will always have drainer people to deal with in life, business and family, but for our own health we need to limit the time we spend with them and manage the influence they seek to hold over us.

So, in what ways can we begin our journey to better self-awareness? To more effectively recognise the possibility that we may be self-centred, a little too proud or a relational *drainer*?

Indicators of low EQ (emotional intelligence) include triggers such as:

- easily getting into an argument.

- lacking in empathy - not being able to understand how others may be feeling.

- not taking responsibility for our own actions and blaming others for *our* mistakes.

It may be that we often feel that *others* are over-sensitive and a little too precious, when in fact it is our problem. Maybe we struggle when it comes to listening and understanding someone else's point of view. Are we able to show real empathy by identifying with the feelings of others?

We don't have to have lots of friends, but having deep, personal engagements with a few people we feel close to is a demonstration of our ability to have **real**ationships. Chuck Swindoll says that you need about 6 good friends in life. That's how many it takes to carry your coffin! If you have identified with one or two of these indicators, you may have a tendency towards self-centredness. If you find yourself in this position, what do you do? You progress and develop by becoming less proud and less self-centred. Many of the ideas discussed in this book, when applied, will significantly help you improve your EQ and help you along the path towards developing **real**ationships – in every area of your life.

> *"Treat everyone with politeness and kindness, not because they are nice, but because you are."*
>
> – Roy T. Bennett

5. Being too pushy.

> *"When you're trying to persuade people, more often than not, they feel you're being pushy. When you focus on influencing them, they're much less defensive and open to hearing what you have to say."*
>
> - MARK GOULSTON

The fifth relational blunder to be avoided – at all costs - is *trying too hard* to persuade someone to do something they are not yet ready for. It is called being *pushy*. If you want to get a short-term win and burn people in the process, being too pushy will deliver a great result – every time.

When I think of pushy people, car sales staff immediately come to mind. (My apologies to all the car salespeople who operate with integrity.) For a brief period in my early 20's, I sold new and used cars. I learnt all the *pushy* techniques for obligating customers into making a choice - on the day, financial arrangements, colour selected, and delivery date agreed upon!

"Would you prefer the blue one – or do you like silver better?" "This is the last one available in that make and colour." "Do you need it before the long weekend - or can you wait until next week?" "How much deposit would you like to leave as a down-payment so we can hold that particular vehicle for you?" I know all the lines and I am sure I myself used some of these pushy sales techniques to get someone to purchase a new car.

When we try too hard it comes across to others as pushy. When we are seen to be pushy, it has a negative effect on the very people we are seeking to influence. People will say no for lots of reasons: I feel uncomfortable, I'm not ready yet to commit to this, I am feeling obligated, I have to check with my Board / Boss / partner, I do not like what you are offering, I need more information, I want to do a background check on how you have looked after your other clients etc.

When we play with a more neutral hand and offer our product, service or partnership in a way that achieves a win-win, it is much easier for the other party to say, "Let's do this!"

A great question to pose after a presentation and discussion is to ask, "Is there anything about this that doesn't work for you?" This makes us completely vulnerable but will open the conversation for the other party to share any concerns they may have. Once that is on the negotiating table, we have a much better chance of meeting our objectives.

It has been said that we tend to buy things from people we like. Why? Because we sense an affinity with them, a connection, the beginnings of a relationship and a level of trust.

> *"I cannot control whether you like me, but I can control whether I am likeable.*
>
> *- Chris Voss*[3]

How do we become more *likeable*? Simply by avoiding these five relational blunders and working hard to learn to listen, learn the art of genuine sincerity, to tell the truth at all times, to be more interested in the other person rather than promoting yourself and by not being too pushy when seeking to reach an agreement. Falling into the trap of one or several of these five relational blunders is could be described by what I call *"the cringe factor"*. The way we physically present ourselves the language we use the jokes we tell, the way we refer to others, our self-deprecating approach to life, where we are genuinely looking out for the benefit of the other. When we do that, we will move us into the realm of establishing *real*ationships that have the potential to last a lifetime.

REFLECTION

Don't touch that! – Five relational No-No's.

Consider the following questions (now or later).

Write down your answers, make notes in the margin of the chapter. Absorb what is helpful for you, jot down some questions

1. Am I a good listener? What can I do to improve my listening skills?

☐ I will try the concept of *'mirroring'* in my conversations.
☐
☐

2. How would I rate my EQ? Am I truly sincere or sometimes a bit of a hypocrite?

☐ Go to this link and complete the EQ test:

https://globalleadershipfoundation.com/geit/eitest.html

3. How often do I tell deliberate lies? What circumstances cause me to do this?

_____

_____

What is it I am trying to achieve by lying?

_____

_____

4. In what ways am I a *drainer* in relationships?

- ☐
- ☐
- ☐

In what ways do I *charge* my relationships?

- ☐
- ☐
- ☐

5. When I think about meeting a goal – how pushy am I and is it effective? What could I do differently?

_____

_____

STEP 5

Inside Out! – Delivering a fresh set of values.

> *"Attitude is a choice. Happiness is a choice. Optimism is a choice. Kindness is a choice. Giving is a choice. Respect is a choice. Whatever choice you make, makes you. Choose wisely."*
>
> – Roy T. Bennett.

Whatever we choose for ourselves says as much about our *attitude* towards life as it does about the circumstances in which we find ourselves. On one of my many visits to Uganda, two young men once approached me asking if they could meet with me. We agreed on a time and met up at a local café.

I sat down with them after buying three cold bottles of Coca Cola, fully expecting that they would request some money or help from me, either personally or from our foundation. When I asked them what was on their minds, they said, "We want your advice about what we should do with our lives."

Now, this was a complete surprise! I leaned forward eager to listen to their perspective and what they had to say. They continued, "We are in our late teens, there is a 75% unemployment rate in our nation and we cannot get any work."

There is no unemployment benefit in Uganda. They wanted me to dispel the myth they heard, that in Australia the government pays people who do not work! A little embarrassed, I confirmed that the rumour they had heard was true.

They went on to describe their living conditions. They were sharing a cramped rented room, which featured a polished mud floor, one small window and a door. They spent their day trying to gather enough food to survive. "We want to know if you can tell us how we can get ahead and make something of our lives?" they asked, staring forlornly at me.

I enquired about their studies, their level of education, what skills they had and what they were passionate about. The response they gave me did not give a lot of scope for a big future for either of them. Keen to affirm them and offer some encouragement, I suggested they do something out of the ordinary.

They needed to change their thinking and get their minds right, in order to achieve a better outcome. I asked them how many of their friends were employed? Their response was, "just a handful of the *lucky* ones." I enquired about how many businesses there were in the area, and they responded, "There are many." I suggested they go to a local business, such as a building supplier, a small-time manufacturer, or a fabricator and offer their services to the owner as a volunteer!

REALationships

I doubt that anyone would turn away the offer of free labour! Once they secured a role, I suggested they be the first to arrive at work in the morning and the last ones to leave each day. They would work harder than all the people who were being paid and give their new boss high quality work for the money he wasn't paying them!

They looked at me wide-eyed and said, "Why would we work for no pay?"

I started explaining to them that we each had 24 hours in our day. Eight to sleep, eight or ten to work, leaving 6 hours to relax, do our household chores and prepare meals (there is no McDonalds or Pizza Hut in Jinja!). While they didn't have work, eight to ten hours a day of their productive time was currently being wasted hanging out with their other unemployed friends, complaining about the lack of jobs!

I threw this idea to them, "If you work faithfully for a month or longer for the boss and one of the other paid employees is always late, steals from the business or is unreliable and gets fired who do you think the business owner will offer a paid job to?"

A look of hope spread across their faces and they both gave me a beaming smile, thanking me for giving them my time – and the Cokes!

I would love to tell you that the story ended up with them both getting full time paid employment. The truth is, I have not seen them since and sadly will never know the outcome of our conversation. However, the principle I was trying to teach them is applicable to whatever circumstance we find ourselves in. We need to get our heads right, change the way we think and push the reset button on the impression we have of life – and the world - in order to get a different outcome for our future. Not surprisingly, excelling in our relationships is one of the keys to living a fulfilled life and making this an achievable reality.

Richard Beaumont

The quote at the opening of this chapter by author Roy T Bennett, in his book "The Light in the Heart"[5] is a poignant reminder that many things in our lives are a choice. The attitude we display is a choice. Choosing to be positive (or negative) is a choice. We can choose to embrace optimism and be respectful of all. It is a choice we can make. Regardless of our circumstances, we all have choices that we are free to make. We may be living in a really difficult situation, but we can still choose the *attitude* we adopt and the way in which we will manage ourselves.

If we allow outside influences to change the way we choose to conduct our relationships or influence our approach and how we act, then we have failed to get our thinking correctly sorted out. When our *inside thinking* changes, that will result in a change in our *outside actions*. It will directly affect the way we manage our relationships and give us the capacity to turn them into **real**ationships.

Many people struggle to manage their relationships. There is no shame in that as it is one of the toughest parts of life in our fast-paced, highly expectant, politically correct, demanding world. Perhaps you are someone who is shy; *'people stuff'* simply makes you nervous. We may feel our language, background, country of birth, education or job role makes us less acceptable, and therefore we do not feel confident in interacting with others. If this is how you feel, don't worry, you are not alone!

I have identified a continuum that starts at *'just plain scared'* right through to becoming a confident *'outstanding relational expert'*. In between these extremes, there is a progression that has the potential to move us from timid, to shy, to nervous, to approachable, to friendly, to confident, to connected through to fully engaged. With a growing sense of self-awareness, we begin to understand *who* we are and how others see us. I believe we can all improve at managing relationships regardless of where we are at. We just need to start the journey of knowing how to be engaged and develop *real*ationships.

Moving from W.I.I.F.M. to W.C.I.C.

> *"Many people want to hang out with you – so long as there is something in it for them."*
>
> - RICHARD BEAUMONT

WIIFM is simply an acronym for *"what's in it for me?"* Sadly, *that* is the main driver of the majority of our relationships. Many people only want a relationship if they can get something out of it. A sexual partner, access to wealth, the right connections, lots of fun, living the high life, a great job, enviable status, an awesome reputation, prestige by association. The list goes on. Most people want to hang out with *you* as long as there is something in it for *them*. The WIIFM acronym is an unconscious descriptor of why I would want to hang out with you. This attitude comes back to the "I" culture that was developed when Steve Jobs launched the iMac in 1998. He says the "i" was a reference to the Internet – a computer that would work right out of the box. Since then, the brand has been developed by some very clever and connected marketers - iPod, iPhone, iPad, iTunes, iCal, iLife, iPhoto and no doubt more to come.

Symbiotic relationships.

In this "*i*" generation, we are driven by what seems to be an obsession with self. We are incredibly selfish - way too often. We are self-serving, self-seeking and self-obsessed. Our cultural norm seems to make life look like a one-way street. All the traffic is going one way – mine. It is all about *me!* Give little or nothing back, just gimme, gimme, gimme! If the basis of any relationship we wish to develop is purely what we will get from it, without being willing to give anything in return, this relationship will only ever be short term. Unless of course the other party sees something, YOU have that THEY want! If that is the case, the relationship becomes parasitically symbiotic. However, not all symbiotic relationships are automatically bad.

Did you know that there are three types of symbiotic relationships?

- **Mutualism** is where both partners benefit: Dogs and humans have enjoyed a mutualistic symbiosis for centuries. The dog supplies protection and companionship, and humans provide food and shelter.

- **Commensalism** is where only one partner benefits while the other is neither helped nor harmed. The cattle egret bird walks amongst cows and buffalo eating the insects disturbed by the foraging cattle, occasionally hitching a free ride on their back. The cattle don't mind but are not helped by this parasitic relationship.

- **Parasitism** describes the gain one party receives at the expense of the other. A stomach parasite feeds well, to the detriment of the host who ends up lacking the nutrients they need to thrive and remain healthy.

If we are earnestly seeking ***real**ationships* in our business life, in our social connections, with our life partner, our relatives, our kids and even our neighbours, then we must change our thinking and move from WIIFM to WCIC – an acronym for **"What Can I Contribute?"** Once we decide in our heads and our hearts, to do all we can to move our key *relationships* into a **REAL**ationship, the key to making this dream possible is to change the expectation we have. Instead of looking for what I can *get*, we must shift our thinking to 'What Can I Contribute?'

So, in what practical ways can we make a contribution in our relationships?

REALationships

I'm privileged to have a lot of really good, close friends. I'm not talking about the 1,010 friends on Facebook, or the 691 connections on LinkedIn. These are all people that I know but only some of them are close friends. I think one of the reasons I have so many good friends is because over the years I have developed an attitude of wanting to *contribute something meaningful* to the relationship and to *serve* others in any way I can. I always try to remember their birthday. If they come to mind, I'll often give them a quick phone call to say I was just thinking about them. If we go out for coffee or for lunch, I always like to be the one who pays (unless of course, *they* have chosen a really expensive restaurant for dinner, which is outside of my budget)! In this case I will at least offer to pay for the wine – but then some of my friends have very expensive taste in wine too!

More than half of my friends do not have a lot materially, they live very humble, sacrificial lives. In spite of their few resources, they choose to invest their time and talent looking out for those they consider worse off than themselves. I am regularly humbled by the people with whom I get to spend my time. Vasgo (not his real name) lives in Mozambique. I have known him for 35 years. He is a pastor, and he and his wife Mary and three children live in a small house in a remote rural part of that extremely poor country. Their existence is very much hand-to-mouth. They grow vegetables on their small piece of land and have some hens that lay eggs.

Vasgo has no regular income. He is the pastor of an 800-member church made up of people even poorer than himself. He and his wife have invested their life serving the community where they live. They help the sick, engage in leadership and vocational training for local young people, and co-ordinate food for the elderly. They also look after widows who get pushed out of their homes by their husband's family when their husband passes away (quite a common occurrence in East Africa).

On my visits to meet Vasco and Mary, I stay in their small guest house – a room in the compound where they live. The water pressure is not great and the only way to bathe is to fill up a bucket with water, stand in the bath with a dipper cup in order to have a '*shower.*' The bed is hard and has a definite U shape to it, so after two nights, my back starts protesting!

One of the ways we like to encourage people is to take them out for a simple meal to a local restaurant. On the second day of my visit with Vasgo and Mary, I was looking for some cold water and opened the refrigerator. I was shocked to find it was completely empty, apart from a very old, wilted lettuce leaf, lying in the bottom of the crisper bin. Each day they had been supplying me with tasty meals – where they were coming from was anyone's guess.

When I realised the refrigerator was empty, I spoke to them and said I would like to give them a treat. We could go out to a restaurant - or would they prefer I just gave them the money to spend so you can buy food for the family? Without hesitating they both agreed that the money would be of more benefit to the family.

Every evening I left several thousand Metcash (a few dollars) on the kitchen bench and every day I was there, we ate well. Mary's kitchen was outside, and she would cook over an open fire in the yard of the compound. On my final evening we were sitting around the fire eating chicken and vegetables. The food was delicious and generous. I asked the family how often they ate chicken and they replied that they enjoyed chicken a couple of times a year. This was a very extravagant, wonderful treat!

Many of my friends in Australia, New Zealand and the US are very wealthy but are also incredibly generous. They support the Entrust foundation and the projects that we identify, such as the education project

REALationships

we fund in the town where Vasgo and Mary live. This is only possible because of the trusted relationship we have built over the years. Many of the donors that choose to partner with Entrust have become my close friends. A number of my close friends have also become partners and donors. Each of these and dozens more are all *real*ationships. Not because of WIIFM (What's in it for me?) but because of WCIC (What can I contribute?)

As I think about my many friends in the West and in developing countries, the way in which I can contribute to our *real*ationship is often simply by being there for them. For some I am a coach. For others I am a mentor helping guide them to provide a local school or establish a much-needed clean water source. Maybe to set up a micro-loan scheme within their community or warn them about the ever-present dangers of human trafficking. They do the work and we help them. Funding is the easiest part of the partnership and when you know them and have built a trusted *real*ationship, donors in Australia are very willing to provide Entrust with the needed funds, based on the strength of our multi-layered partnerships.

Julie and I have just spent a weekend with our good friend Jacky. She lives near a marina full of amazing boats in a beautiful part of the Mornington Peninsula in Victoria, Australia. Jacky's husband, David, was one of the first people I met when we moved from New Zealand to Australia in 1978. Sadly, David passed away several years ago due to motor neuron disease. We all miss David a lot and staying connected to Jacky is something we love doing. She is always saying, "Come down and stay – the place is yours – even if I am not here!" On Saturday, while we were staying, I asked Jacky if there were any little jobs she needed help with around the home. I did some digging and moved some rocks in order to enhance Jacky's beautiful garden. I measured a deck and an area of garden to work out how much material she'd need to order from the local garden suppliers. We had a wonderful weekend together and we tried to do what we could in order to make a contribution, helping her with things she was not able to do on her own.

My ***real***ationships have a widely varying dynamic. There is a huge contrast and difference in location and circumstance between Vasgo and Jacky! I cannot and do not treat all my relationships with the same approach. I have learned to adjust the way I think and work, depending on the circumstances of the people with whom I am relating to at the time. My life often feels a little surreal as my pendulum swings widely from one extreme to the other, sometimes in a matter of a few days or hours.

For all my friends, regardless of where they live or their life circumstance, I try to contribute to our **REAL**ationship by being there for them, encouraging them, helping in practical ways, often being an advisor or mentor – a sounding board for their ideas while encouraging them in their faith journey as well. I realise that for all of these ***real***ationships we are great friends because *their* attitude is also '*What Can I Contribute?*'

Seek First to understand…

Stephen Covey is the author of one of the best and most practical personal development / management books I have ever read, "The Seven Habits of Highly Effective People"[6]. I am sure you have heard of it and hopefully devoured it as I have.

Covey's habit number six is, "Seek first to understand, then to be understood." This is something I have endeavoured to build into my life ever since I first learned the lesson. My approach – wherever possible – is to listen and try to understand where the other person is coming from, before I jump in. I must confess, the most difficult individual with which to apply this habit is my youngest son! But that's a story for another day.

When we spend time understanding the other person's thoughts, concerns and ideas, we then have a framework with which to respond. Seemingly, the only time this principle does *not* work is if the person with whom I am meeting applies this very principle to me, by getting in first! This turns the tables. I get to share what is on my mind so that they can then respond with an answer informed by a clear understanding of the issues I'm dealing with.

It doesn't matter who speaks first. It makes no difference to the outcome of the conversation. What matters is that both parties are genuinely trying to understand the issues and goals of the other and to accommodate them, while looking for a mutually beneficial outcome. Of course, this sort of solution is never that simple and is not always possible. The other party may want something we cannot deliver. We might be after an outcome that is impossible for the other party to help us with.

Seeking first to understand and then to be understood is not a magic bullet. However, it is an effective tool that will help us more than we can imagine when applied with the right mindset. Remember, we need to get our heads right and then our actions will follow. If our attitude and our desire is to be sincere in helping the other person, then the outcome, in many ways, is just a subset of this principle. We may not get what we are seeking, but we will have achieved a meaningful engagement, which may serve us well in our future business or social connections. Winning the deal at all costs is a very selfish (and an "I") approach to life and business. We may win the odd battle here and there, but we will lose the war!

"But then how do I achieve *my* agenda?" I hear you asking.

> *"Without goals, and plans to reach them, you are like a ship that has set sail with no destination."*
>
> — FITZHUGH DODSON

As you absorb the ideas and concepts suggested in this book, you may think: "If I implement what is being suggested, I will never be in a position to reach *my* goals and achieve *my* agenda. I will spend half my life being nice and listening to what everyone else wants!"

We all need goals, and we must have a clear agenda. We need direction and a destination! No one is suggesting we should not have an agenda. The problem arises when we drive our agenda like a bulldozer pushing anyone and everything out of our way so we can achieve our goal- at any cost!

Many of our transactions in life are day-to-day and by nature, we do them in a mechanical fashion. We need to buy food at the supermarket, we need to put fuel in our car, we need to pay the power and gas bills, we need to look after the property in which we are living. In these transactions I am suggesting that we be more aware of others and engage with them in an intentional and meaningful way. That, I promise you, will make our daily chores a lot more pleasant. Remember that attitude, kindness and respect are **choices** we make – every day.

I choose to engage with people at all levels in my life. I believe it is the little things that say a lot about who we are and what we think of others. I've heard of a large company in the US that only employs their senior management team members after the CEO has taken them out for lunch. He will select a nice restaurant and they would enjoy a pleasant meal together. The test the CEO is conducting was to evaluate the way in which the prospective employee engaged with the front-of-house staff serving them. If the potential employee is pleasant and polite to the wait staff, they pass the final test and get the job. If they are proud, rude or off-hand, demeaning those serving them, they are not employed. It all comes back to the culture the corporation wants to have amongst the senior management team. They want leadership that respects everyone – regardless of their role in life.

REALationships

If anyone wishes to reach senior management we must learn to engage in polite and courteous conversation with those serving us in a restaurant, at the 7-Eleven or as we go through the drive-thru. If we do not learn to do this now, there is little chance it will start to happen automatically when we are given the opportunity to lead a large team. In fact, I would suggest that if we don't learn these basic life-lessons, we will never get to lead a team at all. Leaders set the pace through their *own* example. How are you doing at this?

A friend of mine in a senior management role arrives at the office early and "walks to floor" to greet the early comers by name, occasionally stopping to chat but sensitive to those who have immediate work that needs doing. As others pass his desk on arrival he greets them by name too. He keeps a photo organisation chart on his wall so that names and faces are always connected. Everyone matters.

A smile costs nothing and does a lot. It changes my appearance it puts me in a more positive frame of mind, and it tells the person looking at us that we are content. Regardless of how people read us, our muscles can send feedback to our faces and this helps to boost our mood. To say a simple "Thank you" costs nothing, takes no time, but means a huge amount to someone else.

To a pilot as you pass the cockpit and look in the door – "Thanks for getting us here safely." To a waiter, "I appreciate your attention to detail." To a checkout operator in the local supermarket, "I hope you are having a good shift." To the barista who has just made your morning coffee, "Thanks, mate! I can see you take your craft very seriously!"

In leaving a restaurant recently, I walked by the "pass" where the chefs deliver the food to the waiters. I ducked down to make eye contact with the chefs and simply said, "Great work guys, the gnocchi was awesome!" The smile on their faces and the appreciation for the feedback was obvious. It costs nothing to be polite and courteous and make everyone feel great. Once we have learned *that* lesson, it will be foundational in helping us achieve *our* agenda.

> *"A gentle word, a kind look, a good-natured smile can work wonders and accomplish miracles."*
> – WILLIAM HAZLITT

Do we want to achieve our agenda at the expense of everyone else? Do we want to leave a mess and have others clean up afterwards? The point I wish to emphasise is that **real**ationships are an effective, efficient way of achieving our agenda while helping others achieve their goals along the way.

In my capacity as a business consultant, I was interviewing someone for a job last year. They had just finished their fourth year studying electrical engineering. I asked the applicant about their fourth-year honours group assignment which they had to complete over the course of the year in order to graduate. "How did your team work together?" I asked.

"It was a disaster, half of them didn't do what they promised to complete, one person did nothing all year and ended up going out for dinner with his father the night before the assignment was due. The rest of us had to do his part as well!"

Their agenda was to spend a year working co-operatively and deliver a result: research, design and implementation which would produce a proven model by the end of the year.

REALationships

Under this "team approach" concept, it was the team that received the pass or fail. No one was examined by the level of their contribution. The recalcitrant engineering student achieved his goal – he got a pass but did little to contribute. My guess is that many teams in businesses, all around the world, have to work with this level of dysfunctionality. It is said, "There is one challenge in every family." I would extend that principle and suggest there is *at least* one challenge in every *work team* as well.

WIIFM 'What's in it for me?' directly competes with HCIC 'How can I contribute?' Whose agenda are we chasing and how can we reach our goals? When we seek first to understand before we are understood we will learn so much more about the goals of others. That in turn will help us understand the meaningful contribution we can make and, in the process, achieve our goals as well. We need to realise that by driving *our* agenda exclusively, we walk over others and damage relationships in the process. A kind word or learning to engage with a simple smile will open doors that no amount of fast talk and sales spiel will achieve. If we know our destination - if our ship has set sail - we will have goals and the necessary charts to reach that destination regardless of the direction the wind blows, or how hard!

REFLECTION

Inside Out! – Delivering a fresh set of values.

Consider the following questions (now or later).

Write down your answers, make notes in the margin of the chapter. Absorb what is helpful for you, jot down some questions. Pass on an idea to someone else.

1. How am I doing *choosing* the following areas. Score myself: (1 = awful, 10 = brilliant!)
   - ☐ Attitude
   - ☐ Happiness
   - ☐ Optimism
   - ☐ Kindness
   - ☐ Giving
   - ☐ Respect

2. What types of symbiotic relationships do I have?

3. What do I need to do in order to change my thinking from WIIFM to WCIC?

4. Name one person I could approach and offer to mentor?

_____

_____

5. Who could I visit and help by doing something they are not good at?

_____

_____

6. Here is my score on my level of friendly engagement with service staff.

    1 =awful. 10 = brilliant. My Score: _____ / 10.

6. Personal Notes:

STEP 6

Navigating the rocks of relationship.
– Charting a wise course.

> *"Be more concerned with your character than with your reputation, for your character is what you are, while your reputation is merely what others think you are."*
>
> – DALE CARNEGIE

We have been considering how we can turn our relationships into **real**ationships. It commences by *'going about'* - starting with a change of direction. We need to adopt a different approach to the one we are currently locked into. There is fake news in the 21st century and also an abundance of fake relationships. There is no cookie cutter that will work if we are to develop **real**ationships because they are complex at best. Learning to manage vertical relationships is a lifesaver for our sanity.

Selfie-awareness is fundamental in understanding how any relationship works – knowing ourselves and understanding how others see us is life-changing. We looked at five relational blunders that we must avoid in order to stop being a *drainer* and we considered what it means to be a *charger* in our ***real***ationships by building trust through better engagement.

In the last chapter, we reviewed the value of getting our heads right. We thought about the change of attitude that is required on the *inside* (in our heads), which will result in a changed response on the *outside* (in our actions). When we always seek first to understand, before trying to be understood, we will worry less and spend less time focusing on *'what's in it for me'* (WIIFM), and spend more time considering *'what can I contribute'* (WCIC) to this ***real***ationship?

Every relationship has the potential to hurt us. Every relationship also has the potential to develop into a fulfilling partnership that is mutually beneficial to all parties and where the sum of the parts is exponentially greater than anything our individual effort could produce. However, we have all experienced the fact that occasionally relationships can end up on the rocks. It is part of life. And I believe it is important that we acknowledge that we cannot please all people all the time. This advice is attributed to Abraham Lincoln: "You can please some of the people all of the time, you can please all of the people some of the time, but you can't please all of the people all of the time".

When navigating a yacht, you either use a paper chart, or in the majority of cases, an electronic satellite navigation map that appears on a screen. Charts are complex and show multiple pieces of information simultaneously. An electronic device gives a lot more information. It will tell you the depth of the water, the direction you are heading, where the land is, where the hazards are, the location of the channel markers and the speed and direction of the wind.

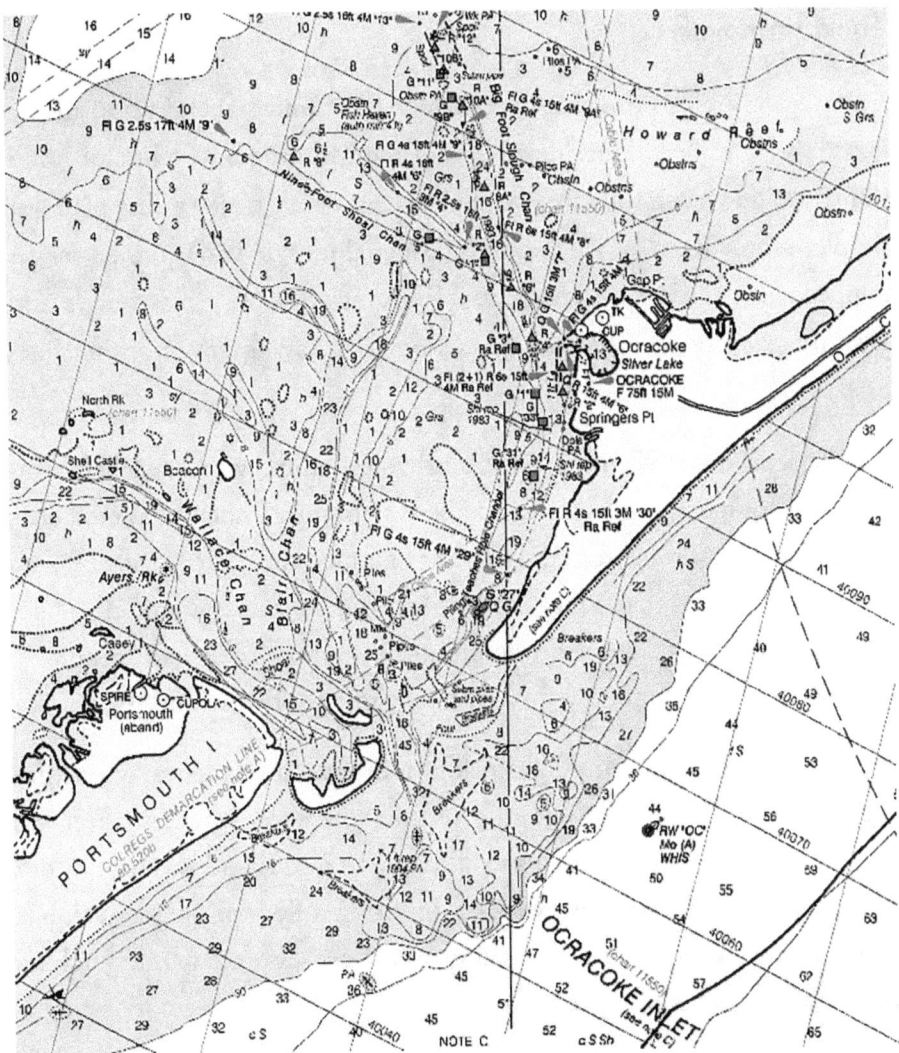

A Navigation chart showing a channel entrance.

One of the many lessons I have learned when sailing is that there are always a lot of things that have the potential to go wrong. I have a theory that once one thing goes wrong, there is usually a domino effect and then a myriad of mistakes seems to pile up on top of one another, compounding the original problem.

Richard Beaumont

The domino effect

A simple example of this theory occurred last summer when I was bringing our yacht, Cavalier, alongside a berth at the Mornington Yacht club. All I wanted to do was simply drop off a passenger off at the jetty. The plan was simple, motor in, have the bow just come alongside while the passenger hopped onto the jetty. Because it was a quick and easy manoeuvre and I wasn't stopping, I made the mistake of not having any mooring lines prepared.

Rookie mistake! Wind, tide and a brief hesitation by the passenger who suddenly got nervous and hesitated about stepping off the untethered boat caused us to drift away from the jetty. As I gunned the engine to get us back alongside, I found that I had managed to run over a stray mooring line, which then wrapped itself firmly around my propeller! I had to quickly turn off the motor and now we were at the mercy of wind and tide.

No engine, no mooring lines ready, and now some metres away from the jetty. The wind was pushing us into shallow water where my keel was about to hit the bottom. All this would have been OK and was fixable, but the most embarrassing aspect was that on the first floor of the yacht club, a dozen seasoned sailors were all looking over the rail, beer in hand, watching my embarrassing predicament!

On another occasion it was New Year's Eve and we were approaching sunset. Cavalier was out in the middle of Port Phillip Bay on our way to a social gathering. I had mis-judged the location of the Great Sands, a vast sand bank that changes with storms and sand movements. The boat shuddered, something scraped below and Cavalier ground to a halt. Keel stuck in sand. The sun was setting and but for a combination of tilting, weight re-distribution and a powerful diesel motor, we could have spent the whole night stuck on the sand bank!

REALationships

The complexities of relationships are not very different to the complexities of sailing. While a glitch may be manageable - and forgivable - the domino effect kicks in and can result in a complete disaster. The interesting thing to note is that these glitches are usually unexpected and often happen as a result of a series of circumstances, few of which may be our fault!

In business, a simple misunderstanding, when it has run its full course, may result in lost business or even getting fired. In a marriage, a disagreement over how to discipline our children can result in learned family values clashing. "My parents always taught me that this is the right way!" Socially, a simple text or email meant as a joke but taken the wrong way and read in a different light can damage connection, understanding and trust.

Our neighbour may set out to poison the ivy on *their* side of the fence and in doing so, end up killing off some much-loved plants on *our* side! "They are deliberately killing our plants – so I am going to do something to get 'em back," could be our knee-jerk response.

One badly improvised impulsive reaction can quickly domino into a series of events that just get worse and worse. Just like my sailing experiences! Mistakes are allowed, but if we fail to manage our responses well, an unthoughtful reaction is rarely beneficial to our relationships. Many of us can attest to the negative consequences of such knee-jerk responses. Instead, let me show you a better way.

The Glue Called Coffee

There is a *glue* which I love and about which I admit to being a self-confessed snob. Yes, I am a coffee snob! I live in the city of Melbourne that has an international reputation for great food and the best coffee in the world! In our multicultural city there are places to go for coffee that will determine how much of a coffee aficionado you are. The *flat white* is a Melbourne invention whose reputation has drifted around the world. I know we are living in a global village when I am in Phnom Penh, Cambodia and I go to Browns Coffee and they understand what a Melbourne *flat white* is!

> *"It's strange how drinking cups of water seems impossible, but 8 cups of coffee go down like a chubby kid on a see-saw!"*
>
> - ANONYMOUS

For me coffee is glue. A social tool that helps me engage with many people from all walks of life. Sharing coffee together equals a safe place. It is not a board room, an office or a formal meeting. It is just having coffee with someone. In a café - a more informal environment. Coffee is the glue of many relationships because it is a wonderful excuse to get together.

The key ingredient in a *flat white* is the actual coffee bean: Arabica, single origin, from the south-facing side of the mountain, grown at the perfect altitude, of a remote mountain in Eastern Uganda, freshly roasted and ground correctly to achieve the perfect *crema*. In fact the Entrust Foundation partners with a village in Eastern Uganda called Mount Elgon, with just the right conditions for great coffee but without the capital to grow and process the perfect beans. Melbournians now enjoy the fruits of their enterprise and children in that village get to eat well and go to school.

There are many aspects to consider when making a great coffee: heating and texturing the milk, ensuring the correct temperature, and a signature *leaf or heart* on the top, all make up the perfect coffee.

When we want to get to know someone better, take them for a coffee. (Make sure you pay – because it says to them you are thoughtful and care.)

A conversation in a more casual environment is a great way to start to build connection and trust. Remember, coffee is really a glue that can help bind our relationships together.

The Poison of False Assumptions

In the earlier examples I gave as to how we miscommunicate and what can go wrong, there is a common denominator: we all assume things. As the old saying goes, when we ASSUME, it makes an ASS out of U and ME. Never assume. We must never think that we know what the other party wants or why they have taken a certain action, or what their motivation or agenda may be.

Just as in coffee, in relationships there are many components. I have come to recognise that the core element is communication. It is only when we are talking to each other, when we are listening carefully, when we are engaged and empathetic, when we are looking at how we can contribute, that true **real**ationships have the opportunity to grow and develop. If I assume straightaway that my neighbour was trying to kill my plants, the approach I may make with them will clearly not be a friendly one. If I believe my business partner or sales staff has done the wrong thing and address the situation by shouting at them and laying blame, I am setting *myself* up for failure. As soon as we accuse someone of something that has not first been verified, we are in danger of damaging the very relationships we need to nurture and thereby giving ourselves a reputation that we do not need, want or desire.

> *"Fools find no pleasure in understanding but delight in airing their own opinions."*
>
> *- King Solomon (Proverbs 18:2)*

So, what do we do when someone does something that offends us? If communication is the key element in any relationship, I believe good communication is also the answer to diffuse misunderstandings.

What would happen if, instead of assuming our neighbour deliberately set out to kill our plants, we took the time out to approach that neighbour? What if we knocked on their door and asked them over for a coffee? What if we then asked them about their garden and how they are enjoying their time making it look beautiful? What if we said that strangely some of our plants had died along the common fence – did they have any advice?

Chances are they will tell us they were poisoning some ivy on their side and it could have been their fault. We then understand it was a simple mistake - they never intended to do it and may possibly apologise! Even if they don't apologise, and although the damage has been done, when we are able to understand each other's actions and hear their side of the story, the heaviness on our heart typically goes away.

An unintended consequence of addressing an issue with kindness, and seeking first to understand, will be to actually build a relationship and open up a chance for dialogue, understanding and friendship. I am amazed by so many stories of people who do not get along with their neighbours!

In a business environment our neighbour may be the person in the next office or at the desk beside us. What if, instead of exploding at our team for what we feel was a rookie mistake, we ask them to tell us what happened. Not to lay the blame, but ask them to consider what they could have done to avoid the problem? It doesn't mean it will undo the mistake, but we will have gained an understanding of that person's heart and we change the culture of our business or team. In my team I often say. "Mistakes are allowed - and are forgivable – just don't keep making the same ones! Always learn from what goes wrong." That is the way we grow.

The importance of tuning in to True North

This leads us to an important principle: what is our motivation for the things that we do? Are we only after making sure everything works out for us, or do we see every situation as a chance to develop our relationships, and eventually, our character? Are we very easily reacting to things in anger because our reputation is at stake?

Character must be the main driver in our motivation, conversation, and decision-making. If we make decisions purely based on our own selfish attitude, or even on what others think about us, we are heading for the rocks. Reputation will take care of itself – so long as we focus on ensuring our character is sound. This has been termed "principle-centred leadership" by Stephen Covey and has become mainstream in the best approach to business and people management. When our compass is tuned to True North, that is our guide - and is non-negotiable.

I have been watching a Netflix series called Ozark. Starting out as a financial advisor for his friend Bruce, Marty Byrde ends up laundering a little cash. Relocating his family to the Ozarks, life and circumstances plummet downhill from this point, to a trail of deception, lies, murder and trying to keep his wife and two children alive, while staving off a ruthless Mexican drug cartel. What starts out as something small and somewhat innocent ends up consuming him and his family drastically changing the course of their entire existence.

The series has graphically reminded me of the slippery slide we head down once we compromise on our core values and we begin to let our principles slip. While Ozark is an extreme example, a little wriggle here, a little compromise there and we can easily find ourselves on a course that will ultimately end on the rocks.

A friend of mine is a lawyer who on one occasion was offered a bulky brown paper bag with cash for laundering. "Only you and me will know about it", the client said. "That would be one person too many," my friend replied.

What does True North look like? Although we may come from very different belief systems, there are certain principles that we can all live by in order to be a positive force in society.

So, what are these principles? This list is not exhaustive, and I could write another book developing each one. Let's think about each **principle** as part of our life compass, that will keep us focused on true north.

- ☐ Moral integrity
- ☐ Pursuit of truth
- ☐ Respect for all
- ☐ Servant attitude
- ☐ High level of accountability
- ☐ Genuine humility
- ☐ Authentic care for others
- ☐ Open communication
- ☐ Admission of mistakes
- ☐ Ability to forgive

When our lives are directed by these (and other) principles, they will determine our character and our reputation will follow. Reflect on my list and see what is missing for you. I am motivated by acting in a way that serves others. I don't expect any accolades because of what I do or who I spend my life helping. It is something that seems to be in my DNA. This is a list you need to establish for yourself – because you will be choosing to live by the principles you select as right for one's for you.

How do these principles affect our response to conflict?

Think about examples of conflict with others in your own life and work. Experts say that the typical human response to conflict can be summed up in three "F" words! Fight. Flight. Freeze. Because freezing is debilitating, I propose we substitute a better word into this combination of three.

Let's have a quick look at each of these responses and consider their consequences.

> **1. Fight:** This is sometimes a good option. If I am being bullied, stand-up to the bully, fight. If I am accused of something I didn't do and I am being unjustly blamed, fight. What should I do if I witness discrimination or see someone being unfairly taken advantage of? Fight - for them.
>
> **2. Flight:** When should we run, or avoid engagement? Several years ago, Julie and I were at the beach. We were walking down a sandy track through some grass to the water's edge. I froze as I saw up ahead a snake laying in the middle of the track warming itself in the mid-morning sun. We didn't take flight, but when I yelled at Julie to stop, the noise was enough to alert the snake to our presence and it shimmied off into the sand dunes.
>
> Removing ourselves from danger or a situation that has nothing to do with us, or where we cannot assist, is sometimes the wisest option. It requires wisdom, experience and a healthy EQ to read a situation and decide on the most appropriate course of action. Walking away is always an option and is not necessarily a weak response.

3. Freeze: This is the response that happens when we don't know how to respond! When driving on an Australian country road at dawn or dusk, kangaroos often get mesmerised by a vehicles headlights and they simply freeze in the middle of the road – often causing a serious accident. When we freeze, it is not a conscious choice we make. It highlights our indecision, our inability to know whether we should fight – or run. How would we feel if the *freeze* option was changed to?

3. Familiarise: This response gives us the power to engage without becoming part of the problem. It allows us to ask a clarifying question, the answer to which may mean we fight or flee! When we familiarise ourselves with a difficult situation, we ask questions that will help draw out the real issue. To go back to our snake for a moment, what if I had asked the question "is this a harmless grass snake or a highly venomous Eastern Brown?" The answer (if I had known) would have helped me make another decision. It would have enabled me to decide whether we stepped over it or do a quick U turn and run!

Start by committing to the 10 principles I have set out in the previous pages. Then when you are confronted with a difficult relationship, your third response changes. It goes from being immobilised - having no idea how to respond-to being confident to familiarise and get more information. A different outcome altogether!

This is how we develop the relational skills required to be respected in our workplace and sought out by others for advice.

No one really wants to fight, but it may be the natural response we always use in order to protect ourselves – possibly due to some history and baggage that we carry as a result. Fighting essentially builds a wall between us and others when we are trying not to get hurt.

Meanwhile, if we *always* run from a conflict, we will likely end up running from problems our whole life and avoid the opportunity to build **real**ationships.

Growing our understanding of relational reality, knowing what our big picture life direction and goals are, is fundamental to a fulfilling and engaged life. We don't want to climb the ladder of success only to find that it was leaning against the wrong wall! While it's good to think about what we want to accomplish in the next week or month, short-term goals can cloud our capacity to see the big picture. I can navigate my yacht by looking just over the bow and feel confident I will not run into anything, while actually forgetting whether I am heading north or south.

Familiarising ourselves with a situation gives us time to build trust and may enable us to start a friendship - instead of forcing others to fight or flee, which is often the knee-jerk reaction many have when faced with a conflict situation.

Do you know what happens when we ask a "why" question? It never gives us the information we need and instead forces the other party into a defensive stand. Statements such as "WHY did you do that?" or "WHY did you say that?" forces people to justify their actions which will often end in tears.

By replacing our almost-habitual *"why"* with *"what,"* we will change the conversation. "*What* was the outcome you were looking for when you did that?" "*What* were you trying to communicate when you said that?"

Note there is no assumption in a *"what"* question. It gives the other person the opportunity to explain what they were seeking to do, without making them defensive.

Where or what is my True North?

> *"My inside self and my outside self used to match. A compass needle pointed to true north. Now that needle spins around and around, indicating the sad direction of nowhere."*
>
> — ELIZABETH BERG

Our True North can become a spinning needle if we forget what is important. There are many occasions when I have encountered a difficult circumstance. Family, staff, colleagues and business associates have all thrown up situations that cause my needle to spin!

For me and throughout my life, I have found that my true north is found because of my belief in a greater power, in a relationship with the creator, the one who made me and created the world in which I live. Without my very personal connection to a faith in God and seeking to follow the profound teachings of Jesus, I would have floundered long ago. I am not suggesting what you should believe. I work with people from all backgrounds of faith and conviction. Muslims, Hindus, Buddhists, Animists, agnostics, atheists, materialists and everything in between. I can only speak for what I have found to be life-changing for me.

Based on the same 12-step principles of Alcoholics Anonymous (AA), Narcotics Anonymous (NA) teaches the principle of putting your trust in a "higher power." On many occasions I have accompanied a friend to NA meetings. At each meeting there is a verbal recognition of the presence of something outside of each of us that is more powerful than we could ever be on our own. NA and AA are not prescriptive about what that *higher power* is, but when we get to the place of recognising that we cannot fix our addictions on our own, only then can progress be made.

Tens of thousands are testimony to the success of this principle and I would encourage you to consider who or what your *higher power* may be. That will help us determine our true north and ultimately our life direction. We will then know where we are heading.

> *"We plan the way we want to live, but only God makes us able to live it."*
>
> - KING SOLOMON

REFLECTION

**Navigating the rocks of relationship.
– Charting a wise course.**

Consider the following questions (now or later).

Write down your answers, make notes in the margin of the chapter. Absorb what is helpful for you, jot down some questions. Pass on an idea to someone else.

1. Look at the summary at the beginning of the chapter. Is there an overall theme that is challenging me as you read this book?

2. Can I identify a relationship that has hit the rocks - where I have been hurt?

3. In what way can I resolve it or put it behind me?

4. Do I regularly have coffee (tea, soda or juice) with others? Can I do it more often and who would I like to better engage with in a more meaningful way?

5. Make a list of the principles I want to embrace in order to keep me pointing true north.

   1.
   2.
   3.
   4.
   5.
   6.

6. Do I have a *higher power* in my life and if not, is this something I should consider?

7. Personal thoughts:

CHAPTER 7

Heart Matters.
– Me, a *Real*ational leader?

> *"People do not care how much you know,*
> *until they know how much you care."*
>
> -JOHN C. MAXWELL

The first six chapters have taken us through six steps of relational change and how we can implement that change in our own lives. Change must start with us – and only then can we begin to become real-ational leaders. The second half of this book will help us work through how to lead relationally, and become confident, effective and successful in whatever endeavour we have set our hearts and minds upon.

*Real*ational leaders set themselves apart from others by showing genuine care for the people they are leading. It does not mean we always have to pamper everyone and be soft and gushy 100% of the time! If we lead real-ationally, our care and concern must come from our heart. This is not something we can conjure up on a Monday morning as we drive into work. When we genuinely have the best interest of our team members in mind, we are also taking great care of our clients and therefore showing great leadership and investing in the future success of our business.

Staging the development of our Relationships

So how do we move from simply knowing someone, to actually being in a **real**ationship with them? How do we know when we have reached that *next level* of engagement in our **real**ationships?

For me it comes down largely to my sense of the **openness** of the relationship. How transparent we are with each other. Are we sharing information that goes *beyond* the level with which we may connect in a normal business or other relationship? Is there honesty and transparency?

Another indicator is what I refer to as *matters of the heart*. Do we feel *freedom* in our communication? Is the **real**ationship a charger (not a drainer)? Is the connection *more* than a business arrangement for me, a means to an end, a way to get what I need from the other party? A heart-felt examination of our true motives will give us clear guidance as to our level of engagement in this relationship.

It is often hard to know when you have *arrived* at a **real**ational level, but I have found it is often much easier to see when looking back. "Ahhh, it was when we had that long conversation about "such and such" that I felt we went from relationship to **real**ationship."

One of my friends is a very savvy investor and property specialist. We have known each other for several years and while we do not see each other socially, there is a great sense of empathy and connection whenever we meet. We had coffee together recently, and he shared with me a number of business thoughts and some personal concerns. When we got back to his office, a client was waiting for him and my friend introduced me to his client. "This is my friend Richard, he runs a foundation, is one of our investors and he is a very helpful mentor to me."

This was the first time there had been an acknowledgement of the type of **real**ationship we had both come to value. It was one of those *looking back moments* when we both realised we had got to the point of verbalising the value we both felt in our friendship.

So how many **real**ationships can one expect to have? The only limiting factor to the number of **real**ationships we can manage is our individual capacity. The principles we have been considering are applicable to our connections at any level, and when applied correctly, will add enormous value to all of our relationships, whether you are a business leader in charge of a small team or the CEO of a multimillion-dollar corporation. Our ability to relate well to all stakeholders, or in effect, the level of our EQ (emotional intelligence), will directly determine our success as a leader.

Naz Beheshti, in writing for **Forbes Women** in 2018, identified that:

> *"Competency research in over 200 companies and organizations worldwide found that emotional intelligence was twice as important as technical and cognitive ability in distinguishing top performers from average ones. In senior leadership positions, it was four times as important."*

Emotional intelligence (EQ) is four times as important than the education or technical skills we take with us into our workplace. If we are in any sort of leadership role, this is a skill we must develop and learn to implement in our daily tasks, if we wish to be effective and make a significant difference in our chosen endeavours.

Richard Beaumont

What are the key ingredients of great leadership?

Many have asked this question and thousands of books have been written on the subject. I do not claim to have any revelations that are not already in print. I just want to explain them in my words in the hope that some will connect with how I think and might get it!

To explain great leadership principals, another sailing analogy will be helpful. There are several important aspects to a yacht. The hull, keel, mast, the halyards, boom, sails and the gear - such as winches, rudder, sheets and pulleys - which make the entire vessel work in perfect harmony.

In life and leadership, we have a similar scenario. Our education, the practical experience we have gained, our EQ and our ability to communicate all converge around our capacity to develop ***real***ationships. Having the capacity for outstanding communication is a common denominator that makes each of these areas work in harmony with the other.

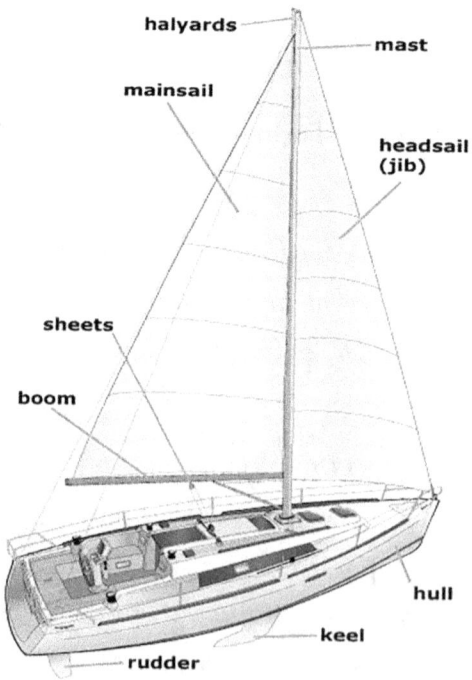

REALationships

The yacht's hull, which is essentially the shell of the boat, could be compared to our education. In sailing, you can have a single hull, a catamaran with two hulls or a trimaran with three. Hulls vary in size, length and shape. They are designed for different tasks – much like the huge number of educational possibilities. We may have a doctorate, a business or accounting degree, or an arts major. What sort of a *hull* do you have and is it suitable for the task you are expecting of it? I would not take an America's Cup boat out for a family Sunday afternoon sail, just as I would not expect a single hull yacht set up for family cruising to win the America's Cup!

We can choose a voyage in life that is suited to our learning or get more learning to take the voyage of our dreams. If we don't have a dentistry qualification, we shouldn't be drilling teeth. If we want to drill teeth, then we need to go to dentistry school. As we live longer lives, we can re-invent ourselves many times and mature age learning is the norm.

The rigging on a yacht is a system of cables, ropes or chains, fittings and stainless-steel stays, which support the mast and boom, essentially holding everything up. Rigging is a bit like our personal life experience. Masts vary in length – some of us are older; many reading this will still be young. The rigging and the experiences we have undergone in our lives hold everything in harmony; our experience enables us to keep going and growing in our capacity. It keeps everything up, ensures our safety and enables us to function with confidence and efficiency.

The sails on a yacht are made of different types of material. They are designed and cut in a particular pattern in order to maximise the power and drive the sail will provide, giving the yacht forward momentum in a variety of conditions. There are many different types of sails depending on the weather and the wind. Sails are the equivalent of our relational EQ. If we have a high level of EQ, we have larger sails and can therefore drive the boat better and faster than someone with small sails - or a lower EQ.

What completes the yacht is the gear attached to every other part of the boat. It is the gear – a collection of many small, seemingly insignificant parts - which enables all the other elements to function in the way they were designed. On their own, no one part works to achieve the goal of moving the yacht through the water quickly, without burning vast amounts of fossil fuel!

A winch, for example, is a cylindrical drum we wrap rope around to give leverage. It enables the sailor to adjust the sail. The winch gives incredible power to pull the ropes tighter and set the sail to its most efficient position providing maximum drive and forward momentum. The pulleys and ropes provide capacity for the boat to be fine-tuned to meet any condition. They enable the sailor to control the sails even under huge pressure from the wind, while harnessing its power efficiently. And of course, without a rudder, the yacht is not going anywhere – with a broken rudder we are simply at the mercy of the tide and wind and cannot harness any of the power and momentum available to us.

Our ability to communicate effectively and efficiently is the **real**ational equivalent of the running gear on the yacht of our lives as demonstrated in our leadership. The winches, ropes, pulleys and rudder - our communication - touches every other aspect of the boat which would be useless if we do not have good communication skills. It is unlikely our leadership will go anywhere without our gear - our capacity to communicate. With no *gear* i.e. poor communication skills, our low EQ and poor relational ability will mean we will drift or be pushed to wherever the wind and tide chooses to take us.

At this point, a quick reminder on communication basics may be helpful stimulus of the varying levels that are present in every connection. The ability to identify what stage we are up to in any relationship will go a long way to help us determine where we need to be – and the goal we are reaching for, which will enable us to attain the next stage.

Five stages of communication.

1. Casual or destructive.

- ☐ A first-time meeting or a conflict within a meeting.
- ☐ The outcome will determine whether we fight, flee or familiarise.
- ☐ If we feel threatened in any way – sabotage is an option.
- ☐ A possibility of dishonesty, lying or exaggeration.

2. Frivolous and ineffective.

- ☐ Information is shared, but not all cards are on the table just yet.
- ☐ Nothing is treated too seriously at this stage.
- ☐ Still exploring, checking out everyone and their motive.
- ☐ May still be using email, LinkedIn or texting.

3. Engaging but factual.

- ☐ Connected but focused on facts – not how we are feeling.
- ☐ Communication is transactional.
- ☐ Still dancing and checking each other out.
- ☐ Trust still not present.
- ☐ Pleasant enough but not yet committed.

4. Cautious and conservative.

- ☐ Starting to share how we feel about the possibilities.
- ☐ Possible pressure to sell or buy the idea.
- ☐ Wanting to obtain engagement.
- ☐ Level of risk is verbalised.
- ☐ Possible negatives are starting to be discussed openly.
- ☐ Ideas are exchanged but resistance may be experienced.

5. Genuine and sincere.

- ☐ High level of trust has been developed.
- ☐ Ideas are openly discussed without fear of rejection.
- ☐ Emotions are shared, concerns expressed, possibilities verbalised.
- ☐ All agendas are on the table.
- ☐ No surprises, and there is transparent communication.
- ☐ Intellectual property (IP) is openly shared and discussed.
- ☐ There is a genuine desire to move forward together.
- ☐ Emotions and interaction are sincere.

*Real*ational follower required!

> *"The pessimist complains about the wind. The optimist expects it to change. The leader adjusts the sails."*
>
> - JOHN MAXWELL

We all broadly fit into one of three descriptors: Leader, follower (optimist) or complainer (pessimist). The only way to know how to be a good leader is to learn first how to be a good follower. Great leaders spend a lot of their energy developing people to become great leaders. Great followers support their leaders and are smart enough to tell the truth in all circumstances. Those who like to complain, the pessimists, are neither leadership material nor follower*ship* material; their negativity will isolate them from those working hard to bring about change and deliver a measurable result. When we find ourselves complaining a lot, let that be the indicator that we are not going to get far in life or business.

A good friend of mine, Harold Seeley AM, always reminded me of this statement, "Those that said it couldn't be done, kept being interrupted by those doing it!" Harold built an impressive manufacturing business and was a philanthropic partner with Entrust. He spent his life getting on and *doing it.* Together with his wife Ann, we were able to partner together working with the poor in Myanmar (Burma).

Today, Ann continues to support the world's poor through her own generosity but also by encouraging two high school students she has known for many years, Mike and Ben, to perform - playing carols at Christmas outside their local supermarket. Over the last 10 years they have raised $10,071 to help poor slum kids in Yangon receive an education.

Mike and Ben are continuing to follow the leadership example set by Harold. I am sure that in doing so, they learned how to become good leaders. Being a successful follower is an under-recognised but important role. Following is a great apprenticeship for whatever may lie ahead. We become great followers by demonstrating a number of traits. One example is our ability to be self-motivated, to deliver what is expected of us. When we follow well, we are being trained for future leadership success.

Five life traits of a successful *follower*:

RESPONSIVE – Learn to listen, seek first to understand, find out what needs to happen, establish the time frame and get on with it. Show the lead to your fellow followers (teammates) by your example.

AUTHENTIC – Be transparent, be genuinely interested in delivering what is needed. Help teammates along the way, don't overpromise, admit mistakes, demonstrate vulnerability, be yourself.

INTENTIONAL – Don't chase shiny things - they are a distraction. Get clarity on the task or goal, ask enough questions to know what you need to do. Engage in minimal research, keep the end goal in mind. Don't blow your own trumpet – remember it is a team effort. Demonstrate generosity in every aspect of the task and be generous when giving out praise for the success of the job.

LONG-TERM – Followers often need to sprint to reach a short-term goal. In doing so, always keep the big picture in mind. Don't win the battle and lose the war! Most of the time there is no "quick fix". Don't use people. Remember **real**ationships last a lifetime - you may be leading them one day.

5. SELF-AWARE – How do I come across to others? If I were the boss, would I trust me? Do I *charge* or *drain* relationships? Am I an easy person to work with? Do I communicate clearly and efficiently? When I walk into a room, do people leave or do they want to engage with me? Do they want to be my friend? If so, why?

It's amazing how much can be achieved when…

A good friend of mine is the son of an Aussie farmer from Western New South Wales. Tom is one of life's interesting characters. He has battled his share of personal struggles but has remained incredibly faithful in investing his life to the benefit of others.

Below his signature on every email he sends out are the words: *"You can get a lot done, if you don't care who gets the credit!"* First voiced by Harry S. Truman, this describes Tom to a "T". Humble, self-effacing, incredibly enthusiastic, always upbeat and positive. He has at least one amazing new idea every day and Tom works hard with his wife Ramona, to bring about long-term change in multiple nations.

What is our true underlying motivation? Why do we do what we do? Is it so we can say *"Look at me!"* Is it so others will respect us more? Pay us more money? Pay more attention to us? Have a higher opinion of us? Realise we are better than they are?

REALationships

Motivation is a *matter of the heart.* Only *you* can assess what truly motivates you and we can only do that by letting down our shutters and looking deep within.

If we are to be **real**ational leaders or followers, we need to come to the conclusion that we can achieve a lot if we *don't care who gets the credit.* The truth is, when we operate this way, we - and those we work alongside - get the credit regardless!

> *"Ever notice that those who whine the loudest, are those who contributed the least?"*
>
> — ANONYMOUS

REFLECTION

Heart Matters. – Me, a *real*ational leader?

Consider the following questions (now or later).

Write down your answers, make notes in the margin of the chapter. Absorb what is helpful for you, jot down some questions. Pass on an idea to someone else.

1. In what ways can I demonstrate to people that I genuinely care?
   - ☐
   - ☐
   - ☐

2. Think of three examples of when I moved from a relationship to a *real*ationship.
   - ☐
   - ☐
   - ☐

3. What are the *three things* that are limiting my communication ability?
   - ☐
   - ☐
   - ☐

4. What must I change to be a more effective communicator?

5. Review the five life-traits of successful followers. Which of them do I do well, and which do I need to improve upon?

6. What motivates me to do what I do? What needs to change?

7. Personal reflection.

CHAPTER 8

Seven Secrets – Thriving team relations.

> *"None of us is as smart as all of us."*
>
> - KEN BLANCHARD

What is your experience of teamwork?

Recently, when I was in Auckland, New Zealand, commonly referred to as the City of Sails, I felt drawn to make a visit to the Viaduct and look at the amazing array of stunning boats. Everything from a 100-year-old wooden classic racer to a 200-metre private motor yacht, that was reputedly a *tender* for an even bigger vessel. Stretching out along the waterfront in Auckland harbour, the Viaduct has been, and once again will be, home for the America's Cup yacht race contenders. It is where people with very big egos – and very deep pockets - will race in January 2021 for the coveted America's Cup trophy.

Richard Beaumont

First launched in 1851, the America's Cup is the oldest trophy in international sport and is yachting's most coveted prize. The trophy dates back to the Great Exhibition of 1851, organised at Crystal Palace in London by Prince Albert to showcase British technology and excellence to the world. A visionary syndicate of businessmen from New York sailed the schooner 'America' across the Atlantic Ocean to represent the United States at the World Fair. The schooner won a race around the Isle of Wight and, with it, a trophy called the £100 Cup. This became known as 'America's Cup', named after the schooner that won this initial race.

The US retained the cup all the way until 1983 when Australia became the first nation to beat America in the race, winning the cup on the yacht 'Australia II' skippered by John Bertrand, against defender Liberty. This win for Australia brought to an end the longest winning streak in sporting history and ended the U.S. domination of the yacht racing series.

Team New Zealand became a household name following their consecutive wins in the America's Cup in 1995 and 2000, under the leadership of Sir Peter Blake, when they initially won and then successfully defended the America's Cup. January 2021 (subject to the Covid-19 pandemic) marks the next showdown on New Zealand's home turf - a decided advantage for Team New Zealand.

As I walked the Viaduct, I was captured by some highlights of the race that Team New Zealand won. It was being proudly broadcast on a huge screen in the Viaduct, boasting their achievement. Over the last 169 years these boats have evolved from classic wooden schooners to incredibly high-tech Kevlar and carbon fibre catamarans, rising out of the water on hydrofoils while racing around a course at 70kph! The teamwork and precision required to keep these boats upright was captivating. There was no individual hero – all had a specific and vital job to do. The task could only be achieved when everyone played their part.

Yes, there was a team leader – the Skipper – but he was only as good as his individual team members – each performing the duties assigned to them. This is a great example of the value of leaders showing genuine care for the people they are leading.

Team New Zealand competing in the America's Cup

Is your team a well-trained, mentally and physically fit, finely tuned machine where each has a role and completes it flawlessly - like Team New Zealand winning the America's Cup?

Maybe your team operates like a university student team I heard about. I was told the sad story during a job interview I was conducting with a graduate electrical engineer, on behalf of a client. It was their honours (4th) year in electrical engineering and in order to graduate, a group of graduate students had to work as a team and complete an assignment together – each doing the part assigned to them to produce an outcome for a team pass.

It seems like the entire team had other priorities! They were selfish, irresponsible, unreliable and lacked motivation while trying to pass on all the hard parts to someone else. One student in particular had done very little to contribute and on the night before they were due to combine their work into one paper ready for submission the next day, decided that dinner, with his Dad was more important! Remember the story of the conscientious and lazy student (at the end of Step 5?) The student who contributed little, but stood up to accept a certificate for a job well done, runs to risk of being excluded from serious teams who value equal effort

In spite of the tension and unfair workload, all were willing to stand up and accept the certificate for a job well done *by the team*, in spite of the fact that they some did little to contribute to its success!

Fifteen years ago, the Harvard Business School conducted research [7] that revealed an interesting insight into the dynamic of workplace relationships. When deciding with whom to work on a project, employees considered two criteria, competence and likeability.

The researchers combined these two measures in various pairings to produce four personality types:

1. *The competent jerk* - knows a lot but is unpleasant

2. *The incompetent jerk* - is both unpleasant and unknowledgeable

3. *The lovable star* - is both smart and likeable

4. *The lovable fool* - is delightful but doesn't know much

We should not be surprised that respondents to the survey said they preferred to work with the lovable star, and that no one wanted to work with the incompetent jerk. Interestingly, people preferred to work with the lovable fool over the competent jerk.

This identified the fact that when selecting their ideal colleague, most people opt for likeability over competence. The researchers concluded,

> *"We found that if someone is strongly disliked, it is almost irrelevant whether or not they are competent; people won't work with them anyway. By contrast, if someone is liked, their colleagues will seek out every little bit of competence they have to offer."*

Change of Course required

These insights further reinforce the fact that we all need to develop our EQ continually if we are to be effective in our workplace and grow in our ability to be a major contributor and an effective partner in a dynamic, high achieving team. Perhaps we need a change of course. If the course we have been on for the last few years has got us to where we are – and that is not delivering - then continuing on the same course can only result in eventual failure.

When we change course – that comes with potential dangers too. We must ensure we navigate the new direction well and with wisdom. Many will refuse to change course even if it means crashing. The unknown to some is more dangerous than the obvious disaster looming ahead. Some people freeze in the face of impending danger (Fight, Flight or Freeze). Changing course with no forethought is just as dangerous – without a plan and some wise counsel we may inadvertently beach our boat and end up stuck on the sand.

Beaching is never the end; we just need to wait for high tide and re-float, hopefully without too much damage. A change of direction could also mean we could end up hitting the rocks and stop suddenly – smashing everything in the process, where there is nothing to recover, and we lose everything with nothing to salvage. Worst-case scenario is that we get hit by a super-tanker in the middle of the night and not even know what happened!

A change of course, a fresh direction and a new approach are essential if we are to remain vibrant and relevant in our marketplace. In March 2020 when Covid-19 became a reality in Australia we were all a bit shell-shocked. As businesses were required to shut down and people sent home to work remotely or receive a 'job keeper' payment from the government, some of us were thinking about what the world might look like for the next few months. What would happen and what does a post-Covid world look like?

As I write this we are still right in the middle of this pandemic. One thing I do know is that the world will never go back to *"the way it was"*. If we are not able to read the times in which we live, assess the effects of the pandemic (short and long term) and be nimble enough to chart a new course, businesses will not survive in a post-Covid world.

On September 11th, 2001 I watched on my television two planes flying into the World Trade Centre twin towers. It seemed surreal at the time. Like a bad movie. Only it was live, real and happening. I remember turning to my wife Julie and saying, "Tonight, the world has changed forever. This day will be a pivot point in the history of the world." And it was. The Covid pandemic, I suggest, will have an even more profound effect on the way the world operates from 2020 onwards. If we are willing to take the risks required and adjust our course, to adapt to our new circumstances, we are in a safe place. If we expect life will go back to normal, normal is not achievable any longer.

Hear the warning bells - 4 signs of weak team relations.

Apart from open conflict, what are some of the more subtle indicators to look for that alert us to weak team relations and the fact that a change of course is needed?

1. *The blame game.*

We blame others for failed projects, not reaching deadlines or bad outcomes. We find it hard to admit our own mistakes and find it easier to point the finger at everyone else. The *blame game* is about as effective as calling a team meeting and throwing a hand grenade into the room! There will be a loud bang and a lot of flak, and *everyone* will get hurt in the process. We will make our point – but the damage will be catastrophic.

2. *The martyr syndrome.*

"Why am I the only one holding this whole thing together?"

"I've been let down by David again! He always stuffs up and is completely unreliable – I had to fix up his mess *again*!"

"Why is it so hard to just do it right the first time? Did you notice the spelling error on page 15 of the report – how could anyone miss that?"

The *martyr* feels constantly let down by everyone else. Of course, *we* are perfect, and we never put a foot wrong – it is everyone *else* that gets it wrong! The standard we set for ourselves is never met by others and we feel that pain. But we also feel compelled to tell everyone what is not right – what was not done perfectly – to *my* high standard!

What we fail to realise, is that in doing this, we are making sure everyone knows how great we are. We forget that in doing so, we are setting *ourselves* up for exclusion, gossip and frustration from others. We unconsciously build around us an environment where mistakes are not allowed – or at least never admitted! If we don't build into our teams the concept that *'mistakes are OK – just don't make them twice,'* we will limit creativity. There will be no room for stretching beyond our comfort zone. If failure is not acceptable, we will smother out-of-the-box thinking that should have put us ahead of the competition and we will stop our team from taking measured risks.

3. Interaction with others is unpleasant.

Some people don't look forward to going to work because there are some very unpleasant people they have to work with. Team relationships can deteriorate from indifference and dissolve into angry discussions, which invariably leads to arguments. If we come to the realisation there is a high level of frustration in much of what we do, we need to examine the way we interact with others and review the quality of our relationships.

We must learn how to turn interaction from *'we just don't get on'* to *'we actually understand each other and enjoy working together.'* Some of the ways we can do this have been discussed earlier in the book.

4. Lack of trust in the people you work with.

Because someone let you down three years ago, you have never trusted that person again since. You overheard a team member make an unflattering comment about their colleague – so they cannot be trusted by anyone.

This indicator reminds us of two things: first, how we behave affects our own reputation and whether others will have a good (or bad) opinion of us which in turn reflects the quality of our work.

The second is that lack of trust highlights the importance of showing some grace and empathy to others. We need to be big enough and mature enough to be willing to forgive people who may have made a mistake, said the wrong thing, took us the wrong way and even hurt us in some way. We need to give trust to others – allow some room for growth and demonstrate that others are able to trust us.

> *"Trust is the glue of life. It's the most essential ingredient in effective communication. It's the foundational principle that holds all relationships."*
>
> - STEPHEN R. COVEY

Seven Secrets

There are not many secrets anymore. Whether you are a 'celebrity' with a million followers, or *Sue Normal* with 50 LinkedIn friends, most of us will know of any scandal within minutes of it occurring, anywhere on the planet. In fact, we can often watch it live on our phone as the news or a disaster unfolds before our eyes. We live in a world with a 24-hour news cycle that never stops.

So, here are seven *secrets* that we likely all know in our heads but probably don't always know how to put into practice. If we implement these **real**ationship *secrets* into our daily lives, they *will* help us build rapport and develop more effective team relationships with our work colleagues. In fact, these *secrets* will help us more effectively engage in *every* area of our lives.

1. Remember a person's name – and use it when addressing them:

Saying "Hi" in the lunchroom is one thing. Saying, "Hello, Richard, how are you doing this week?" can open up an entirely different conversation. In Australia, we substitute a person's name for the affectionate term: "mate". It is often an attempt to hide the fact that we have forgotten a name. But it denies the uniqueness of the person we are engaging in conversation.

2. Listen long, talk short:

Practice using our newly developed listening skills, mirror what others are saying to us by repeating 2 or 3 keys words. "You are really worried…" "Mmmmm frustrated…" "You enjoyed that…" It is important to be impartial but supportive.

3. Ask about *their* story:

This is not an elevator conversation, but the time will come when it is appropriate to ask, "So tell me your story – I am really interested." Be sensitive to gender when doing this – we need to be careful our interest is not perceived as 'hitting' on someone or that we have an ulterior motive.

4. Verbalise your appreciation for them / their work / their passion:

Say something to pay them a (genuine) compliment. And don't 'bang on' about it by going *over the top* in your praise, because that can often come across as insincerity.

5. Stay genuinely engaged in the conversation:

Focus on them, nod, acknowledge, engage. Don't be distracted by your phone and don't look at your watch or over their shoulder at the screen behind them. Try to recall what they told you the last time you spoke and bring it into the conversation. Ask a follow-up question. "Is your daughter OK after her operation?" "Did you do anything special on your holidays?" "How did you enjoy Fiji?" It is OK to help your memory by jotting down things of interest. I heard of a dentist whose clinical notes included what he talked with the patient about at the last appointment. Although I still find it difficult to have a conversation with a suction hose stuck in your mouth.

6. Look for reasons to say thank you:

Be sincere in your praise. "You did a great job on that assignment – it made it so much easier for me to give my presentation to the management team. Thanks a lot!" "I noticed you cleaned up the board room after our meeting – I appreciate that." No one needs a speech, but a simple thank you goes a long way to build relationship and grow trust.

7. Demonstrate you care, by offering to help in some way:

I am a great advocate of 'servant leadership.' We must demonstrate the sort of behaviour we expect of our team, by willingly serving them and helping them. I enjoy being the barista and make coffee for everyone at our Wednesday team meeting. I occasionally pick up the mail from the Post Office if I am in the area. I try to help out in lots of little ways. Why? Because that is what I expect of each of my team members!

Check the chart

When sailing in unfamiliar waters, a chart will tell us most of the things we need to know. Last year I was sailing solo from Williamston near Melbourne to Port Arlington at the southern end of Port Philip Bay. It is a harbour I had never been to before. I needed to know which way to enter Port Arlington, how deep the water was, if there was a strong current I should be aware of, which berth I could use, and should I tie the boat up to the dock bow in or stern in?

I had to check the chart. I made my plans and just prior to arriving checked the chart again to refresh my memory. What I saw on the chart helped me make sense of what I saw as I sailed towards the port.

A really simple but helpful management tool that will help team *real*ationships thrive is to *check the chart* by asking our team members two simple questions.

1. What are your priorities this week?
2. How can I help?

The first question helps *them* focus on what is important, while giving us a heads-up on what they are focused on. The second question gives our team members an opportunity to express their expectation of *us* and tells us what *we must do* to help them succeed in their work. This is gold! When we *check the chart* of our business or team, on a regular basis, we stay connected to the things that are important. We know exactly where we are, the conditions we are dealing with and what is going on.

Navigate by judgment, cultivate accountability through REALationship.

Does your car have a satellite navigation system? Mine does, but the car is now 5 years old – so is the map! In the last 5 years, freeways and roads have changed. There is a new tunnel here and a new road there. As you depart Melbourne's airport, the freeway options have undergone major changes due to road upgrades. If I follow my old *'sat nav'* I am guaranteed to go the wrong way and completely miss my exit. If I follow the new signs that have been erected and do what they say (blind trust), I end up in the right place.

Navigation can be done remotely but the most effective way to navigate is by carefully observing what we see around us. A sign, saying *'Exit Here'* may mean some road works up ahead that requires me to slow down, or an accident that has closed off a lane may force me to merge unexpectedly. If I choose only to obey the verbal instructions from my five-year-old sat nav map, I would get lost, break the law and possibly have an accident!

In teamwork, navigation is best done by judgment. We need to trust our team to observe the conditions around them and navigate the way forward, trusting that they will see the hazards and judge their response appropriately. Sitting in my Melbourne office while trying to micromanage partners in another country will never work effectively.

In the organisation I run, we have decided to allow our overseas implementing partners to navigate by judgement – theirs. This demonstrates to them that we have full trust in their ability to judge local conditions and prove our trust is warranted. We build relationships, we put in place broad boundaries, we set a budget and key performance indicators (KPI's), and then we let them navigate locally – because we trust them.

It is just not smart for me to sit in my office in Australia and instruct our partners in Asia how to run their anti-trafficking organisation, suggesting the best time to raid a local brothel that we know is selling underage girls! Careful surveillance, knowing which police they can trust, working out the best timing and when the owner will be present so they can be arrested – is not something I could even begin to do from Australia. We give them the freedom and empower them to *navigate by judgment.*

Think about how you may apply the principle of *navigation by judgment* with the team you may be part of – or the team for whom you are responsible:

- ☐ What needs to change?
- ☐ How will you implement that change?
- ☐ What will the change do to team dynamics?
- ☐ What is the best way to communicate the changes?
- ☐ What do you expect will be the impact?
- ☐ How will you manage any fall-out?
- ☐ How can you ensure successful implementation?
- ☐ What can go wrong?
- ☐ How will you mitigate that risk?

Does this mean our partners can do whatever they want with our funding? Absolutely not!

Accountability through REALationship is the second part of this principle. Transparency and accountability are mandatory in all our partnerships. Our partners' accountability is not the "master/servant" or "donor/recipient" model that I often see when people in the developing world are receiving resources from Western funders. We are partners with shared goals and expectations standing shoulder to shoulder each doing our part for the good of the whole.

Accountability is managed because of the trust relationship in which we have jointly invested. This means frequent communication, the occasional Zoom call, regular visits, faithful reporting and above all, complete honesty and transparency.

If you decide to introduce to your team the principle of *accountability through relationship,* go through the same list of questions and write your answers down. Any lofty *'principle'* is nothing more than a nice idea - until we decide to enact it.

Dealing with difficult people.

> *"I know ... I don't HAVE to be this sarcastic, but the world has given me so much material to work with ... and I'm just not one to be wasteful!"*
>
> - ANONYMOUS

A discussion of thriving team ***real*ationships** would be incomplete without addressing the issue of difficult people. It is not a case of asking if you know one – more likely the question should be *how many do you know* or have to work with?

Every family has one or two members who present a *'challenge'*. Every business has their share – sometimes it's the boss! There is always a difficult client that we can never please. So how do we manage them and turn someone who is difficult into a more pleasant work colleague or business connection? The truth is, for some, you can't and won't – because they choose to be difficult and have a narcissistic/manipulative personality. It is unlikely they will ever change.

According to psychologist George K. Simon, successful psychological manipulation means the person doing the manipulation will ***firstly*** conceal their aggressive intentions and behaviours. ***Secondly***, they will find out the vulnerabilities of their victim to determine what tactics are likely to be the most effective. ***Thirdly***, they will use a sufficient level of ruthlessness and have no qualms about causing harm to the victim if necessary.

Consequently, the manipulation will most likely be done in a very subtle way. They will either be *relationally* aggressive – causing harm by damaging someone's reputation or *passive* aggressive – giving an indirect resistance to the requests of others while avoiding direct confrontation.

There are three simple ways we can start to deal with difficult people. There are no easy answers or quick fixes, but these will serve as a basic guide:

1. Identify *who* is causing the problem and assess if you are overreacting or making it something it is not. If you feel there is a real issue affecting you …

2. Take the concern and discuss it with a trusted colleague or friend *outside* of your workplace or family. (Outsiders are generally more objective and less politically motivated.)

3. If at least one other trusted person confirms your concerns, approach the difficult person for a *private* conversation. Be gentle, non-accusatory and questioning in your approach. Use an *'I'm trying to understand'* attitude. Express your concern asking how they see the situation from their perspective. Ask if they have any concerns and hear them out. Ask how you may be able to help them, then ask if they could help you.

The reality is that sometimes they just have to go. Employers reflect that they hired too fast and fired too slow! I've had to fire a few people and it is never fun. If we take time to reflect on the hire that goes wrong, it is worth stopping to recognise the indicators we observed and ask if we should have seen it coming earlier?

An article by Kathleen Eisenhardt published in The Harvard Business Review reported on a study which found that the teams with minimal interpersonal conflict were able to differentiate between personality issues and work issues. These companies had six tactics in common for managing interpersonal conflict:

1. They shared commonly agreed-upon goals.

2. They resolved issues without forcing consensus.

3. They maintained a balanced power structure.

4. They worked with more information and debated on the basis of fact.

5. They injected humour into the decision process.

6. They developed multiple alternatives to enrich the level of debate.

REALationships

This gives us good insight into where we need to focus in order to minimise conflict in our workplace, family or even at our golf club. We all need clear direction. We want to see issues resolved while allowing for freedom of opinion. We understand the importance of clear roles and a balance of power, we focus on facts, love having fun and develop lots of options to stretch our thinking.

> *"Courage is what it takes to stand up and speak. Courage is also what it takes to sit down and listen."*
>
> — SIR WINSTON CHURCHILL

REFLECTION

Seven Secrets – Thriving team relations.

Consider the following questions (now or later).

Write down your answers, make notes in the margin of the chapter. Absorb what is helpful for you, jot down some questions. Pass on an idea to someone else.

1. Write down 5 things my team does well:

    - ☐
    - ☐
    - ☐
    - ☐
    - ☐

2. Write down 5 things my team could do better:

    - ☐
    - ☐
    - ☐
    - ☐
    - ☐
    - ☐

3. List three of the 'seven secrets' I will start working on.

- ☐
- ☐
- ☐

4. What are the two questions to ask my staff – that will help my team thrive?

- ☐ What …..
- ☐ How….

5. How would I implement the principal of *navigating by judgment and accountability through* **real***ationship* into my work, social or family life?

6. Personal reflections:

CHAPTER 9

Effective. Authentic. Radical.
– A fresh approach to client relationships.

> *"Success usually comes to those who are too busy to be looking for it."*
>
> – Henry David Thoreau

After developing selfie awareness and learning how to build *real*ationships with our teams, let's now look at how we can improve the way we manage client *real*ationships.

The term *'client'* has become so overused that it has diminished the value of its original meaning. That is, a relationship of guarding and protecting another. When a lawyer accepts a client, the lawyer pledges to guard and protect the client's interests. In current usage, someone who is a client is in fact a customer – one that we serve or to whom we offer our services. If you are receiving an unemployment benefit or getting assistance from social services, you are referred to as a *client*. When I was much younger, a *client* was a significant person or large business paying huge amounts of hard-earned money to an expensive and exclusive law or accounting firm, for their prestigious legal and tax advice.

What do we call the people we exist to help? Customers, clients, partners, donors, supporters, colleagues, punters, consumers, the public; these words describe those who will purchase our products or services. They may be internal consumers or external but each of them has a name – they are in fact human beings. Every enterprise, office, business or organisation exists to help someone - in some way, shape or form. For our purpose I will succumb to modern idiom and we will use the term *client*. But always with the "flavour" of serving and protecting- not exploiting. As we explore the subject of better managing client relationships, you can apply the term you prefer to your own unique situation.

Regardless of what we think success looks like, in my experience, it often comes when we least expect it. Success can pop its head up from left field – as Henry Thoreau states above – when we are too busy to be looking for it. Or as Thomas Edison put it: "Opportunity is missed by most people because it is dressed in overalls and looks like work.

The other observation I have made about success is that how we achieve it is often counter-intuitive. The harder I have tried to *"sell"* something to a client, the more elusive the sale seems to become. Expensive handmade crystal, real estate, vehicles, IT services, investments and even community development projects all need clients – people whom we serve - to make the activity a success.

The key to managing client relations is directly linked to our individual ability to engage and communicate with the people we are trying to help.

REALationships

We can work for a prestigious law firm and people will initially accept us by the reputation of the legal practice. If we turn up badly dressed, not able to engage with the client and our communication style is ineffective, they will be on the phone before we have left their carpark, looking for our replacement.

I am sure you have heard the expression that *customers buy from people they like*. The truth is, this statement is just plain wrong. Customers actually prefer to buy whatever they need from people they **trust!** This principle applies to everything from the supermarket we use for our daily food requirements, to those from whom we purchase a car, a service for our business or even the travel agent who books and helps us plan our annual holiday.

In Australia two major supermarket chains use a very different approach. They are both selling FMCG (fast moving consumer goods) but one has a tag that says, *'The fresh food people'*. The other is a challenger brand and makes the claim, '**Good. Different.**'

Woolworths is promoting trust by stating that their food is fresh, while also introducing a human element. The other is Aldi – a German-based company offering stock on pallets, self-packing, low prices and multiple random household offerings every week. They are building trust by warning people they are different but promising that the experience will be good if we shop there. We don't usually buy from people we *dislike*, but if you think about it, the majority of our purchases are bought from people we trust. Although we may not think about it, this even includes our local pizza place! If the place looks a little unkempt, the people are not friendly and the pizza is good one day but terrible the next – they will lose out trust. We will find an alternative pizza joint that is clean, friendly and makes awesome pizza – every time!

Domino's recently developed an app that takes a photo of the actual pizza you will receive before it hits the box and is delivered. They are trying to build trust by *showing* you how good the pizza is even before it arrives at your door!

If we make our daily purchasing decisions based on who we trust, then any decision bigger than a pizza purchase or our weekly shopping expedition must have a much stronger element of trust attached to it than we would probably care to realise. If trust is the key in our client relations, what does that say to us about the value of the way in which we present ourselves, our ability to effectively communicate and the value of developing a **real**ationship with them?

Networking is 'old school'

I walked into a function room and was confronted by 45 people, all of whom were attending a small business 'networking' event organised by a local business group. We were allocated a number and I had 2 minutes to make my business pitch to another person. I then had to listen to theirs. Ten, 2-minute presentations later I was over it! I had to move from person to person, talking then listening, evaluating their pitch and assessing whether or not their offering was even viable - let alone anything in which I was remotely interested. I did meet a couple of interesting people that evening, but the rest of them were nothing short of awful!

I hate… detest… seriously dislike… networking! Did I make that clear enough? Old school networking is where you walk into a crowded room of wannabe hopefuls, with a pocket full of business cards to meet people whose unreasonable expectation is that they have a product or service that everyone else in the room is desperate for.

Sometimes before the first sentence is even exchanged you are already looking over their shoulder to see if there is someone else in the room that may be a better fit. Surely there is *someone* here who is of more interest than the tedious bore you got landed with. The only thing on your mind is, "How do I extract myself from this conversation – quickly?"

There are multiple ways to 'network'. It may be a cocktail party, social drinks after a conference, or a special event to put similar people in the same room. It may even be an internal business event where you are trying to "sell" yourself or your services to another department. Maybe you are spruiking an internal transfer. In most cases it is the same pattern. Name? What do you do? Who do you work for / which department? Are you any good at what you do? Tell me a hero story! What is your USP (unique selling proposition)? All these questions have an underlying agenda and that is inevitably W.I.I.F.M - what's in it for me? Or, if I am a little more gracious, is there any synergy between us? Rarely in these circumstances do we ever think W.C.I.C. – what can I contribute?

Building a network vs 'networking'

At the risk of overstating my position - I hate networking but thoroughly enjoy meeting interesting people – even if there is no WIIFM. In fact, if we focus on the W.C.I.C., we would find people far more engaging and we would get a lot further in our engagement with them.

There are many varied ways of engaging with people in a business setting. To be effective we must first consider their situation and understand their world from their perspective. What is the problem *they* may be trying to solve? How can I assist them in that endeavour? It may not directly help our situation, but it will give us a good opportunity to make a meaningful connection with them. This will often lead to those first steps needed to build trust.

If you want a quick fix, perhaps you should buy a lottery ticket. Building a network is very different from networking. Being effective in building a network is a life-long pursuit where our goal is to build trust which eventually leads to forming **real**ationships. This is an effective long-term way of placing ourselves in a position where others will trust us, and where we will be credible, helpful, well connected, and willing to assist, regardless.

To aid our capacity in building client **real**ationships, I have developed an easy acronym to remember: E.A.R.—and yes, it's also a good reminder of which sense organ to use the most!

        E – Effective

        A – Authentic

        R – Radical

Adapting to stay EFFECTIVE. (E.A.R.)

> *"There are those who make things happen, there are those who watch things happen and there are those who ask, 'what happened'?*
>
>   – Robert T. Kiyosaki

Where do we rate ourselves on the Robert Kiyosaki scale? Do we make things happen? Are we proactive and do we intentionally take up every meaningful opportunity that presents itself? Maybe we are a little more conservative or shy: we sit back and watch what others do; we don't want to jump in too fast. Maybe we are not early adopters of anything new, but our style is more aligned to: "let's just wait and see what happens."

Don't get me wrong – I am 100% for measuring what we take on, looking at risk, thinking through the implications, consulting with others who have more experience etc.… but I never want to be in the camp where we are seeing change all around us and asking, "What happened?"

REALationships

Two poignant examples of *"What happened?"* in the business world are Kodak and Nokia. At one point in history, both were outstanding leaders in their field.

Kodak had firm control of the film and print market. The trouble was, they did not foresee the impact of the digital world, which was coming at them like a freight train. Steve Sasson was the Kodak engineer who invented the first digital camera in 1975. In presenting his invention to Kodak's corporate management, their reaction was, "That's cute—but don't tell anyone about it." [8]

Kodak eventually conducted a study to look at the impact of digital photography, the results of which produced both "bad" and "good" news. The "bad" news was that digital photography had the potential capability to replace Kodak's established film-based business. The "good" news was that it would take some time for that to occur and noted that Kodak had roughly ten years to prepare for the transition. Their problem was, during the 10-year window of opportunity, Kodak did little to prepare for the inevitable disruption!

Nokia is another sad tale. It is one of complete lack of vision, of scared middle managers who couldn't tell their bosses the truth, and of arrogant top-level management who wouldn't listen. In October 1998, Nokia became the best-selling mobile phone brand in the world. Their operating profit went from $1 billion in 1995 to almost $4 billion by 1999! They manufactured the best-selling mobile phone of all time, the Nokia 1100, which was created in 2003. I used this model myself for several years and loved it!

By the end of 2007, half of all smartphones sold in the world were Nokia. In the same year, Steve Jobs introduced Apple's iPhone. Apple had a meagre

5 per cent share of the global market. It took Nokia 3 years to develop their "iPhone killer," which failed to match the competition. In just six years the market value of Nokia dropped by about 90%. In 2013, Microsoft acquired Nokia, which they struggled to make work and then on-sold the business. Meanwhile, in 2018 alone, Apple sold 215 million iPhones, and held a 47% share of the premium smartphone market segment!

It sounds like the CEO and Board Members of Kodak and Nokia all woke up one morning and asked, "What happened?"

There are many lessons for us from these two stand-out examples. It is often said that hindsight is a wonderful thing. It is too easy for us to look back and see all the things that were done wrong and pass judgment on their stupidity. It is much more difficult to be effective in the moment and choose wisely from the options that are before us - options that can decide our future success, or failure.

> *"You only have to do a very few things right in your life so long as you don't do too many things wrong."*
>
> - **Warren Buffett**

We must be AUTHENTIC. (E.A.R.)

I have a confession to make. I have become increasingly intolerant of fake stuff. Fake hair. Fake tans. Fake handbags. Fake clothing. Fake news. Fake advertising. Fake competitions. Fake marketing. Fake food. Fake prizes. Fake TV shows. Fake 'stars.' Fake people on reality TV shows. Fake people in business. Fake people in any sales role. Fake people who ask, "How's your day going so far?" as I pick up a morning coffee! It's 7:30am for goodness sake - my day has barely started!

REALationships

What is it about our fascination with fake stuff? Why is it so important to look the part without the price tag? Why does my email box fill up with spam telling me I have won a competition, when all they want is my email, telephone number, MasterCard and possibly my first-born child – in order for them to send me the prize?!

If we are serious about building **real**ationships we must reject the temptation to take the fake path and instead develop a genuine, authentic approach. I happen to own a (high quality) fake IWC watch. The $7,500 price tag for the genuine one was a bit eye-watering for me. The $50 fake model was not to pretend to be something I am not – but to have some fun with a good friend who has a real one!

Banning pretentions in our lives is what will help us become genuinely more authentic. Please do not even think about it, let alone try and be something you are not. I have always tried to be open, honest and transparent - even if it potentially hurt my opportunities. People can *smell* fake a mile away, so I was never going to get that opportunity anyway!

Authenticity is based on who we are and what we stand for. The words we use are only a reflection of what is already embedded in our heads and hearts. If we don't like who we are inside, it is next to impossible to achieve behavioural change until we get our heads and hearts aligned with our core beliefs and life-values.

> *"Authenticity is more than speaking; authenticity is also about doing. Every decision we make says something about who we are."*
>
> – SIMON SINEK

Richard Beaumont

On Being RADICAL (E.A.R.)

I enjoy anything to do with water – swimming, sailing, surfing, snorkelling. When we were kids, our family would visit a local river and swim in the freezing water that ran straight off the snow-clad mountains in the South Island of New Zealand. Floating lazily down the Waimakariri River on a rubber inner tube was lots of fun. However, when we got to a certain point in the river, we were not allowed to venture further and had to jump off the float and swim back upstream, so we could do it all over again.

The principle of *swimming upstream* is something that has stuck with me in the way I seek to develop **real**ationships. It's easy to do things the same way as everyone else. But to be predicable is unimaginative and for those on the receiving end, quite boring. While making sure I am not over-stepping a boundary I always try to be real with people. I always attempt to *swim upstream* by engaging with others in a way that will be memorable for them.

This can be as simple as helping clear the dishes when we are at someone's place for dinner. It may be asking them a *'left field'* question that others are too embarrassed to ask. A question such as asking the name of their indoor plant? Can you recommend it for me? Because my gift is killing them – not growing them! It may be asking people what their motivation is for their generosity. It could be sending someone an old-fashioned post card or making a phone call to say you were thinking about them today and wondering how they are doing.

Julie and I were driving past a home we used to own and noticed a For Sale sign on the house next door. We had a great relationship with our former neighbour, Dawn. I would help her trim the hedge between our two properties from time to time and bring her rubbish bins in if she had forgotten. Julie would drop in and have a cup of tea with her and pick up any shopping she might need.

When we arrived home after our drive, Julie called Dawn's daughter, because Julie had made friends with her as well. Enquiring after Dawn, we were told Dawn had passed away 6 months prior. Julie passed on our love and condolences and reminded her daughter how much we enjoyed our friendship with her Mum. You may be asking why we would even bother. Authenticity is a choice, it is who we are, it is about connecting and allowing our actions to be reflective of the values we hold dear. When we do these sorts of things we are swimming upstream – being truly authentic. Authenticity is always about putting others first – never me.

Chasing a "Win-Win"

> *"In a negotiation, we must find a solution that pleases everyone, because no one accepts that they MUST lose and that the other MUST win... Both MUST win!"*
>
> -Nabil N. Jamal

The concept of 'win-win' has been around for a long time. Sadly, many people do not understand it – or want it! The mindset still exists that says, "I do not want to lose face." "I do not want to show weakness." "I do not want to give any ground." "I want to dominate this market at all costs." "I must maintain my margin."

Being radical in a negotiation and looking for a win-win will not require us to get angry. We may need to set boundaries - take a punch and maybe give one back. Keep in mind that the person we are talking to is not the problem; the situation or deal we are talking about is what is important.

Chris Voss in his book *Never Split the Difference* [3] suggests some excellent questions to use in a negotiation:

- What is the biggest challenge you are facing?
- What is important to you about this?
- How can I help you make this better for us?
- How would you like to proceed?
- How can we solve this problem?
- What is it we are trying to accomplish?
- How am I supposed to do that?

It is important to note that each of these questions is a *what* or *how* question – not *why*. As I've mentioned earlier in this book, a *why* question will often trigger a defensive response, whereas a *what* or *how* question will open up dialogue and enable disclosure. As we work through these types of questions in our negotiation, looking for a *win-win*, it is obvious to the other party we want a fair solution, not an "I win, therefore you lose."

Managing clients by engaging in ***real**ationships* will require three things from us:

First, we must be committed to be **Effective**, which means we need to adjust our sails to suit the wind of the market – and not be a Nokia or a Kodak.

Second, we must be ourselves – our **Authentic** selves—and commit to remaining transparent and honest as we progress in the relationship.

Thirdly we need to be **Radical** – to swim against the flow, to be different from everyone else. Sure, it requires more effort to know how to ask the right questions that will get us a win-win. However, this approach will make us radical and ultimately stand out.

> *"Whenever you find yourself on the side of the majority, it's time to pause and reflect."*
>
> – MARK TWAIN

REFLECTION

Effective. Authentic. Radical.
– A fresh approach to client relationships.

Consider the following questions (now or later).

Write down your answers, make notes in the margin of the chapter. Absorb what is helpful for you, jot down some questions. Pass on an idea to someone else.

1. How can I use the information in chapter 9 to develop better client **real**ationships?

- ☐
- ☐
- ☐

2. How does the principle that *'clients only engage with people they trust'* reflect the way I conduct my:

- business
- team
- sales force
- marketing
- HR department
- entire organisation

3. What can I do *now* to future proof my organisation and prevent myself from becoming a Kodak or a Nokia?

4. In what ways can I be more:
- ☐ EFFECTIVE
- ☐ AUTHENTIC
- ☐ RADICAL

5. What can I do to encourage / promote / actively engage / achieve a win-win for me and my clients?

CHAPTER 10.

Shift Happens – Agility and the speed of change.

> *"If I'd asked my customers what they wanted, they'd have said, 'Don't change anything.'"*
>
> - HENRY FORD (1912)

Everything is changing – at break-neck speed! It is increasingly harder not only to catch up, but to keep up. When I got my first computer, it was *dial-up* and, in hindsight, so slow! I could send an email (of sorts) to my colleague 800 kilometres away at no cost and I thought this was cutting edge! Change - and fast change - brings with it some fall out, so shift does happen!

My good friends and Entrust partners have developed an amazing strawberry farm in South East Queensland. 'Taste 'n See' strawberries are the best in Australia. They are big and luscious. They not only look good, they taste amazing! My friends now use drones to fly over the farm, dropping micro-organisms that eat any bugs that attack their 1.2 million strawberry plants – without causing any damage to the fruit! The drones are quick, efficient and provide a huge cost savings to many farmers. They have lifted their plants off the ground onto waist high frames. This is much more efficient and assists with the back-breaking work of harvesting. They are constantly adapting.

A wind shift:

There are so many things happening around us, affecting our daily existence – and we have no clue about them. To highlight my point, here is a list of 15 things that the speed of change in our world is already delivering or working on in 2020.

- The camera on my cell phone is now as good as my expensive digital SLR camera.

- Mobile phone apps continue to be developed, effectively placing all the services that a local bank branch can offer right in our pocket.

- Feeding money into a parking meter is a thing of the past. I am now registered with 'PayStay' and I only pay for the time I use – all billed automatically to my credit card.

- It has become *normal* to talk to machines. 'Hey Siri / Google / Alexa… turn on the lights, send a text, tell me the weather, call mum.' Refrigerators, TV's, lawn mowers and vacuum cleaners are all being manufactured with voice control and (very) remote control through my phone.

REALationships

- Farmers' new tools now include solar equipment, soil sensors, drones and data analytics all designed to maximise farm productivity. Combine harvesters are guided by satellite.

- Sports highlight grabs are being packaged and brought to us instantly, using artificial intelligence (AI), courtesy of IBM's supercomputer nicknamed *Watson*.

- The concept of *Blockchain,* an open, distributed ledger that can record transactions between two parties efficiently and in a verifiable and permanent way, is enabling cryptocurrency transactions, as well as many other things, in the financial world.

- Architects, builders and designers have taken 3D to the next level and are now using augmented reality (AR) to map and measure building interiors. It allows them to completely digitize their world and *'walk'* a client through their new home. This transforms every step of the building process.

- Our legal system is undergoing a revolution due to AI which will quickly search through reams of data, so that the lawyers can spend more of their time personally interacting and crafting strategies with clients, instead of sifting through reams of old case files and legal rulings.

- 350,000 drivers in Canada have saved 10% - 25% on their car insurance costs by allowing their driving habits to be analysed by an in-car device. This measures the way they drive, thus proving who is safe and who is at higher risk of an accident.

- Travel by hyperloop – a pod-like train that can travel at near-supersonic speeds inside a futuristic airless glass tube – is still years away. However, instead of spending 1.5 hours in an aircraft (four hours actual travel time) flying between Melbourne and Sydney, (880kms) the hyperloop could potentially do it door to door, in a comfortable 51 minutes.

- Customers have already developed a taste for ordering food digitally, ahead of time and using home-delivery apps. This is forming a significant part of any restaurant's bottom line. Covid-necessitated takeaways have transformed the food delivery business.

- Cable-less magnetic levitating elevators will be able to move vertically and horizontally, taking up less space in a building and going twice the speed.

- Companies are already using AI to select their future employees. Algorithms have the capacity to look beyond degrees, experience and other basic resume material to predict a good fit for a future employee.

- Small businesses are operating without cash registers. At the Australian Open Tennis Tournament, the only way to buy food is with a card – no cash allowed. We are fast moving to a cashless economy as physical cash is considered 'risky' in a Covid-world.

Purchasing a $1.00 coffee at 7-Eleven with a card was OK. In fact, many businesses did not accept cash during lockdown and this trend has continued. Cash has become 'dirty'.

Of the 15 items listed, I wonder how many of them you were aware of? My guess would be less than half of them at the most? With everything around us changing so fast, the need to engage in *realationships* is even more important.

With AI doing more of the hack work than we ever thought possible, relationships will be increasingly essential to allow meaningful connection with each other.

Checking conditions - adjusting our course:

A good sailor is an alert sailor. They will be aware of their surroundings, have an eye on the weather, know how to read the clouds and look for the wind ripple coming across the water – before it hits the sail. I can see a gust of wind coming simply by observing the way the surface of the water is moving when looking at the water around me. I will know where it is coming from and how strong the gust will be. I am prepared when it hits the sails a few seconds later. When sailing I constantly check the conditions, and when necessary, adjust my course to suit the conditions as they present.

In today's world we place an ever-increasing reliance on apps, computers, data, machines, chips, social media, likes, surveys, bots and analytics. We are bombarded with multiple points of influence – a deluge of information telling us what to do, when to do it and how to manage our lives, our businesses, our teams, our friendships, our families, our households and our day-to-day living.

Our major anchor that will enable us to navigate the future world will be *real*ationships. They will be our way to connect and engage emotionally so we can debate, develop, have our thinking stretched, engage our emotional intelligence (EQ), and be real. In fact, without *real*ationships, we are simply breathing processors! To relate well to each other - and emotionally connect - will be the only way we can remain truly human.

We must be confident and capable in our ability to develop and maintain meaningful person-to-person interaction. We don't just want to connect; we need to understand. To interact. To share our concerns and to achieve business and life outcomes in the way in which we are designed. Relationally, in deep meaningful, connected, heart-felt *real*ationships.

> *"The world as we have created it, is a process of our thinking. It cannot be changed without changing our thinking."*
>
> — ALBERT EINSTEIN

The wind never blows from the same place all the time. It is affected by tides, the moon, temperature, currents, humidity and seasons. So, let's not worry about the fact that life will change. Instead, let's work out the best way to accommodate the change whilst staying the course of our lives and thriving in the vocation we have chosen.

My career path has been an unusual one. I have engaged in a huge variety of activities, been in a wide range of situations and travelled internationally for work my whole life. I have often said, "I never want to die wondering…" I wonder what would have happened if I hadn't taken that risk? I have always been willing to embrace risk, try new things and grab hold of every opportunity afforded to me. Would there be some things I would do differently – of course. Did I learn a lot anyway – you bet!

Non-negotiables in the midst of change:

Then again, in the midst of all the change happening around us, what is one thing on which you will not compromise? What are our absolutes, the things we will never let go of? I am sure you could write a list and I believe it would be helpful to put them on paper. Have you ever stopped to think what it is you would be prepared to die for?

In the early 2000's, I was managing a business for an Australian manufacturer, running their state office. We had a service team, dealer network, retail sales and a team of representatives all working to look after the business. It was high stakes and we worked hard to maintain the company's excellent reputation. The State I was managing was providing over 60% of the manufacturer's Australian income.

I had a boss in HQ, 800 kilometres away, who was telling me what he thought our customers needed without really being connected to the local market and not always being willing to listen to the viewpoint of those on the ground. The business owner is still an amazing, passionate and a true innovator. We had some internal challenges that were slowing my sales potential down and, in my view, were not being addressed fast enough in a very seasonal business. I was a little frustrated and was pushing back on several fronts with several people at the same time. Andrew was an external consultant who was engaged by the business owner to look at what was happening and make some recommendations to the board.

I will never forget the day Andrew walked into my office and said, "Richard, I want you to pick the hill you want to die on." He went on to explain that I could not keep fighting the system on multiple fronts, manage everything they expected of me and fix all the other issues at the same time. In essence, he was saying, *'Make a choice.'* I was asked to pick the one thing that would add the most value to the business, and that which I felt passionate about; the hill I wanted to capture - the one I was even prepared to die on if necessary.

That experience taught me many things and I valued Andrew's coaching and the owner's advice on many occasions. What was the issue on which I was not willing to compromise? Many of us are placed in situations like this regularly. When do we negotiate, compromise and seek out a win-win in order to achieve a goal or outcome - and when do we decide to dig in? What are our non-negotiables? What are the issues of morality, personal choice, integrity, reputation, truth and honesty on which we stand? Which way is our moral compass pointing? What is the hill on which we are prepared to die?

I have an amazing wife, Julie. We have been married for 45 years and we have walked life's journey in harmony together. Has it been easy? – not at all. Have we made some unwise choices? – without doubt. Have we learned from them? – I hope so! Even as I write this, I am preparing to leave Australia tomorrow for 10 days' work in Asia, visiting four countries, on six flights, meeting with many local people – in the midst of the 2020 Covid-19 pandemic that originated in China in Dec 2019. Am I going to cancel? No way. Am I going to be careful? You bet!

Shift happens and life cannot go *'on hold'* because of changing circumstances. Unless we have the ability to embrace change, be aware and able to detect the *'wind shifts'* of life and know the times in which we live, and unless we can adjust our course to suit the conditions that surround us, we will become irrelevant and be left behind.

For me, the anchor, the non-negotiable is my commitment to meaningful engagement and connection with others. This is an area in which I cannot and will not compromise. I always seek out a win-win. I check my motivation - to make sure I am not just in it for myself. I search for a WCIC (what can I contribute?) If we do not embrace these principals, we will not be able to grow and develop and keep pace with change. Because shift happens.

> *"Life is change; Growth is optional – choose wisely."*
>
> - KANDYSE MCCLURE

REFLECTION

Shift Happens – Agility and the speed of change.

Consider the following questions (now or later).

Write down your answers, make notes in the margin of the chapter. Absorb what is helpful for you, jot down some questions. Pass on an idea to someone else.

1. How many of the 15 items mentioned in the list of recent innovations was I aware of?_____

2. What does my answer reveal about how well I am keeping up with change?

3. Am I willing to *adjust my course continually?* If so, what is it that may stop me?

4. What can I do to remain flexible?

5. What new opportunity have I embraced in the last 3 months?

6. List 6 things on which I am not willing to compromise:

1.
2.
3.
4.
5.
6.

7. What is my hill that I am willing to die on?

8. Personal Reflection:

CHAPTER 11

Tacking into a head wind Effort well rewarded.

> *"To reach a port we must sail, sometimes with the wind, and sometimes against it. But we must not drift or lie at anchor."*
>
> — OLIVER WENDELL HOLMES, SR.

We are sailing towards our goal. We know where we are going, what we are doing and with whom we are doing it. It has not been an easy voyage, but we have learned a lot along the journey. The high wind that would have bothered us a year ago is no longer a threat. Navigating the rocks of our relationships, we have a quiet confidence that we know how to engage with others and achieve a win-win result and do this by developing *real*ationships. Our hearts have been stirred as we have read and considered how we may continue this course of our lives, confident in our ability to be much more ***real***ational in our approach and manner.

When we want to sail directly to where the wind is coming from, the laws of aerodynamics and physics make that an impossible task. The way sailors achieve that goal is to "tack" or zigzag into the wind. Imagine a clock. The wind is coming at you from 12 o'clock—which is exactly where you want to go! Oops, how in the world do you sail towards the wind? When sailors tack, we point towards 10 o'clock for some time, then zigzag cross to 2 o'clock, then back to 10 o'clock. It is a bit slow, but we eventually reach our destination.

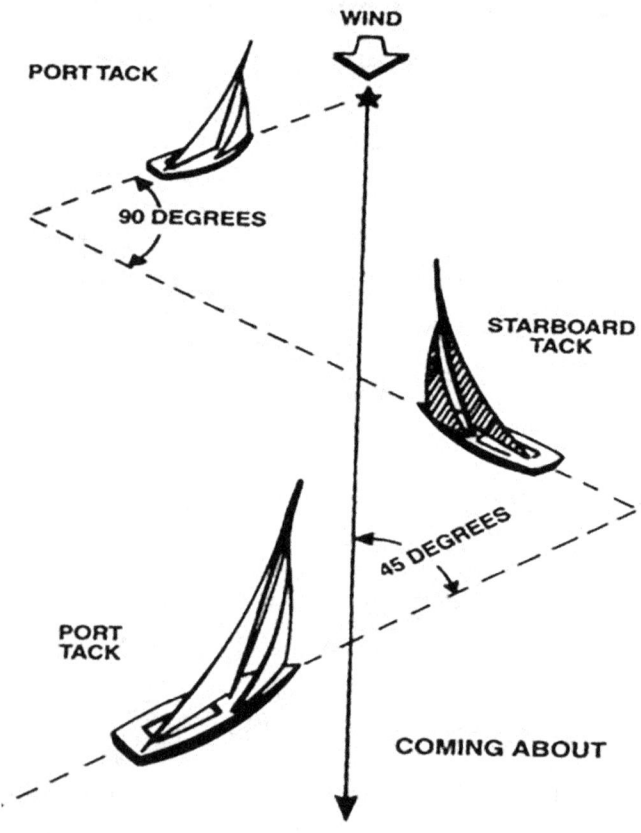

REALationships

Tacking can be hard work and you can get quite wet doing it, with the wind and waves coming straight at you. Arriving at our destination gives us an appreciation that we have beaten the weather and the waves and got there regardless—and a real sense of satisfaction. Going into the wind is effort well rewarded.

If sailing is a metaphor for life, then some of our lives will need to be spent 'tacking.' We can't directly head to where we want to go – because moving from high school to CEO is not going to happen. We have to tack to university, then tack to some actual business experience, then tack to a leadership role. We have to prove our capacity to those that will move us into greater areas of responsibility. You are getting the picture I am sure. We are heading towards our goal – but it is not a direct pathway.

If we constantly *hear* of some great ideas or *read* about them in a book or magazine and we fail to *act* on them, after a while we become immobilised and will no longer be able to hear, let alone act. The reasons I included a *'Reflection'* page at the end of each chapter is to help you do just that. Stop, think, reflect, act. If you haven't used the reflection page – go back and tackle one a week for the next 12 weeks. You will be glad you did.

Change is an often uncomfortable but a necessary part of stretching, growth and human development. It is said that our ability to change reduces with age. Older people are often quite set in their ways and their capacity to adapt or adjust to the new world in which we constantly find ourselves diminishes with time.

I was recently invited to my close friend John's 80th birthday party. (It is such a privilege to have a close friend who is 80 years old!) Not to flatter him – because his ego will not manage it well, but John doesn't look anything like 80! I am sure - if other events are anything to go by - he will turn up at his birthday party in a floral shirt, bright red pants and a pair of trendy yellow shoes. He will have a full head of grey hair, a drink in hand, a big smile, a warm welcome a sarcastic quip about me - but always a compliment for my wife, Julie.

John has spent his life keeping up with what is happening, staying young, and engaging with a wide variety of people. He has a broad circle of friends and an equally broad, generous heart. We have travelled together to some of our Entrust Foundation projects and his heart was broken to see the way others live. He has chosen to make a difference, and he and his partner Rosie are wonderful friends and a huge encouragement to us. John has kept up with the speed of change and is alive and loving life as a result. There are others I know who seem to have aged before their time.

I would encourage you to determine with me, that keeping abreast of change, maintaining a flexible and open attitude will keep us tacking towards our goal. Let's determine that we choose NOT to allow ourselves to be held back by the challenge of the task at hand.

A life-long perspective

Just as John is a great example of a **real**ational person who does not allow age to get in the way or slow him down, it is important that we each take a *life-long* perspective when it comes to how we manage and maintain our connections.

I have sought to remain engaged with some of the people I grew up with. There have been many influencers who speak into my life, and for that I am extremely grateful. The founder of what is now called the Entrust Foundation, Eugene Lincoln Napoleon Veith, was one of those people who took a life-long perspective.

Eugene's early recollections were as a small boy living on a farm in East Gippsland in rural Victoria, Australia. Walking 4 miles (6 kilometres) to school each day with a father who was not the best farmer in the district but a man of generous spirit, Eugene learnt to be content and generous. He recalls a guest coming to stay at the farm and leaving the children threepence each, as a small gift under their pillow. (About 3 cents in today's currency).

Eugene told me he thinks God gave him a generous spirit. Saving his money until school was finished for the week, Eugene decided to spend his gift on the Saturday, he walked the 6 kilometres into the local town and visited the corner store. His 'threepence' enabled him to buy 4 chocolates. Clutching the bag of chocolates, Eugene then turned and walked the 6 kilometres home.

"How many chocolates do you think I still had in the bag when I arrived back at the farm?" He enquired of me. Shrugging back at him, I suggested he ate 3 and kept one spare. "Four!" was the response he gave, accompanied by a big smile. "I didn't eat even one on the way home. However, I did give three away to my family members and enjoyed one myself - it tasted delicious!" Eugene's generous spirit was already being exercised.

In the mid 1930's Eugene's family moved back to Melbourne and started a butcher shop during the great depression. Giving away more meat than you sell because you feel sorry for the women who could not afford your sausages, will never become a *best practice* model for a successful business. Eventually, Eugene's father went broke and the only asset the business was able to rescue was a tired Austin 7 delivery van with a missing front door.

Eugene would often tell me, "At 22 years of age, I had hyalophagia (no hair) and a bad stutter. I actually thought I was a *no hoper!* People must have felt sorry for me," he added, "because they gave me a job asking me to help them move some boxes from one location to another. I did it quickly and efficiently and I kept on being asked by others to help them with parcel deliveries."

A long-term legacy…

Eugene took a long-term view of life and business. He quietly went about his work, building **real**ationships and trust, delivering on what he said he would do, engaging with his clients while enjoying his work and the connections he made along the way. The stutter eventually disappeared as his self-confidence grew. He purchased a toupee to cover his lack of hair and slowly built his business, giving away a lot of the profits to help his brother who was a missionary in India.

There were two major department stores in Melbourne at that time that were in fierce competition, Myer and David Jones. Eugene was able to navigate the fine line of serving them both and making them each feel important. By now he had several vans and worked out that if you put a roller blind on both side windows of the van with different logos on them, you could adjust your advertising to suit the client. When he turned up at the Myer Emporium loading dock, they saw the Myer logo in Eugene's van window, as would the customer when he pulled up outside their home to drop off the parcel.

However, when David Jones Department store called him for a pickup, Eugene would roll the blind around until the David Jones Logo appeared! Each business thought Eugene had delivery vehicles exclusively working just for them!

Roll the clock forward to the mid 1980's. Veith Transport is now the largest parcel delivery business in Melbourne with over 300 taxi trucks, vans and contract drivers. Eugene just drew a wage and the profits from the business were given away to worthy causes. Eugene once told me, "In a good year, some of my best contract drivers would earn more than me – and I owned the company!"

Veith Transport was sold in 1986 when bank interest was returning 18%. Eugene said it was easier to invest the capital than run a complex parcel delivery business. For the next 22 years Eugene and his board gave away 50% of the income generated from interest received on the capital from the sale of the business and put the other half toward growing capital. The funds at that stage were in a trust. Eugene had in effect, given all the money away and would not take anything for himself.

We estimated that in his lifetime, Eugene had distributed around $23 million to those that needed it far more than he did. I will never forget the brief conversation I had with him when he was already 94 years old. He was genuinely concerned he would not have enough money in his personal savings account to cover the cost of his funeral! "I don't want to be a burden on anyone after I go," he told me.

It was my privilege to have known Eugene for 35+ years and he was such an encouragement to me on so many levels. It is also my privilege to be able to lead the organisation he started, which continues to thrive today - to champion the burden Eugene had to help the poor, the widows and the orphans in the parts of the world that few others even know exist. Eugene Lincoln Napoleon Veith took a long-term view of life – and his view is still impacting the world, long after he has left us.

… or a Short-term grab.

When we take a long-term view of life and business, it forces us to change our approach, to adjust our sails for the conditions we are currently encountering. Many corporations in the USA, indeed much of the US economy, seem to be driven by quarterly profits, income projections, interest rates, international indices and consumer confidence. Of course, these are some of the metrics the market uses to work out where it is headed, but it has a downside.

This management style forces us to think short-term. It forces us to grab some quick sales, delay capital expenditure and bring on staff lay-offs to meet short term goals. Often for no other reason than to achieve the handsome incentive bonuses and rewards paid out to CEOs and senior management. Sometimes it is an effective strategy and drives our businesses forward but there are other times when it damages the long-term goals and strategic viability of the business. The short-term grab mindset often results in paying a heavy price in the long run.

I do not do any *'fund raising'* for our organisation. I have learnt not to go for the short-term grab. Money is donated to Entrust by people who get to know us and who we also want to get to know. Some have been referred to us, some we already knew and still more stumbled over us. All the while my goal is to help them achieve what *they* want. I am not in a hurry, I make sure people know what we do, how we do it and offer to help them achieve *their* philanthropic goals. If we can help them via Entrust – we do. If they want to give to an area we do not work in, I will help them identify someone they can trust. This is one of the ways I have taken a long-term view of life. **Real**ationships enable us all to reach our goals.

Heading for Hobart – and not just the first marker

The Rolex Sydney to Hobart Yacht Race is an annual event hosted by the Cruising Yacht Club of Australia. The race starts in Sydney, New South Wales and finishes in Hobart, Tasmania. Starting on Boxing Day each year the yachts, large and small, race over a distance of 1,170 kilometres. The smallest yacht last year was just 30 feet long and the largest, Comanche, was 100 feet. The Sydney - Hobart is widely considered to be one of the most difficult yacht races in the world due to the variable weather and a crossing of Bass Strait, which separates the island state of Tasmania in the south, from the Australian mainland.

The first race in 1945 was originally meant to be a cruise between Sydney and Hobart with a group of friends. However, when a visiting British Royal Navy Officer, Captain John Illingworth, suggested it should be a race, the event was born.

26th December any year, regardless of where I am, I try to get to a TV or, if necessary, watch a live feed on my computer. As a sailor, it is always fascinating viewing. There are two key moments to watch for. The starter's gun is the time when all boats have manoeuvred (read: pushed, shoved, and manipulated) their way, using all the rules of racing, to get to the prime position and be first across the start-line when the gun is fired to signify the start of the race. The 170 entrants all head east up the harbour towards the open sea and are focusing on the first marker. Once reached, they will turn at the marker and head due south, with Hobart set firmly in their sights.

But guess what? Being first across the start line and having the good fortune to be the first boat to round the marker has nothing whatsoever to do with who will win the race! You see, the race has a longer-term goal; it is not about the first 30 minutes (short term goal); it is about who is the best navigator, which skipper has the ability to read the weather conditions, to maximise their boat's capacity, speed and agility - and stay off the rocks. These attributes – along with a multi-million-dollar yacht, is the edge that will help determine who wins the race.

What sort of race are *we* running? Are we pushing and shoving to get first across the start line and first around the marker, or are we heading for Hobart, with a long-term view in mind? Are we willing to go the distance and become a **real**ational player like Eugene – a self-confessed "no-hoper"? In my view he won the race. He took a long view and made the world a better place along the journey. Thinking about what is *really* important is a cathartic moment in life. Are we content with what we have? Are we willing to invest in people and causes that are way bigger than our little business or corporation?

It is not an either/or question. We do not have to sacrifice one for the other. Many businesses have proven we can do both.

Are we heading for Hobart - or just for the first marker?

REFLECTION

Tacking into a head wind. – Effort well rewarded.

Consider the following questions (now or later).

Write down your answer, make notes in the margin of the chapter. Absorb what is helpful for you, jot down some questions. Pass on an idea to someone else.

1. Recall a time I have tacked into a 'head wind', got to my destination and felt rewarded by my effort.

2. On a scale of 1 – 10, circle where do I think my life-long approach currently sits.

Short-term: 1 2 3 4 5 6 7 8 9 10 Life-long:

3. What are the Advantages and Disadvantages of adjusting my perspective to Life-long?

<u>Advantages</u>   <u>Disadvantages</u>

4. What are the short-term **grabs** I am currently chasing?

5. How will they best serve my long-term goals?

6. Is there something I would like to do in my lifetime and leave a legacy - such as Eugene's? If yes, what could that be?

7. Personal notes / reflection:

CHAPTER 12

Set the spinnaker - Using our skills to streak ahead.

> *"If you can't fly, then run. If you can't run, then walk. If you can't walk, then crawl. But whatever you do, you have to keep moving forward"*
>
> - Martin Luther King Jr.

One of the most difficult things to do in sailing, is to set a spinnaker. At least, it is for me. This is the largest but lightest sail. Often multi-coloured, it fills with wind coming from the stern of the boat. When raised, a spinnaker moves the boat at the same speed as the wind. You have the impression there is no wind. It produces a very quiet and calm atmosphere onboard. We are sailing *with* the wind. However, keeping the spinnaker up is often a more difficult task, especially if the wind decides to move and comes at us from a different direction.

In yacht races, working the spinnaker efficiently often means the difference between winning and losing. When we set our spinnaker quickly and efficiently, we soar. If we get it wrong it has the potential to capsize us, wrap around our hull, fill with water and tear or pull us out of control, straight onto the rocks.

Relationships are a bit like the spinnaker of our lives. When they work well, we soar. When we get the spinnaker wrong, it can cause untold damage. A novice sailor doesn't get to use the spinnaker on their first day on the water. It is important that the novice sailor learns the basics of sailing and has those worked out first. Then, as their confidence and experience grows, as they observe how the more experienced sailors operate, they learn what to do and how to do it.

The quote from Martin Luther King at the opening of this chapter, reminds us of just that. We do not need to worry that we are not yet experts in developing and managing our relationships. For me, it's a long game and I take a life-long approach to learning. I started out with a crawl and progressed from there – but I did keep going and growing and I now feel quite comfortable *'flying'* in my ***real***ationships.

Let's conclude by reviewing the steps we have learned

1. We decided to *"Go about"*.

We need to realise when it is time to *'go about'* – to take a different direction from the one in which we have been travelling. If we don't change, we get more of the same. We have evaluated, changed direction and we are on a different course. It felt uncomfortable at first, but we are seeing change taking place all around us. It feels great!

2. We have discarded the cookie cutter.

We understand that every one of our relationships is unique. We are not allowed to use a *cookie cutter* approach to any of our relationships. We must treat each new connection and every relationship individually. Fake relationships (along with fake news) are no longer a part of who we are. We are real, authentic and transparent. This will enable us to change and develop many of our existing relationships into ***real***ationships.

3. We have developed our 'Selfie' awareness.

We know ourselves better because our *'selfie awareness'* has been fine-tuned and is now a part of who we are. We recognise how we come across to others, we are consistent with every engagement and connection and because of that we are comfortable with what others may say about us when we are not there. If it is negative, we don't care because our compass is pointing us to our true north. We know who we are and the values that drive us.

4. There are things we don't touch!

We are now aware of the *relational blunders* we can fall into when we connect with others. We have learned to listen, we are not self-centred, we tell the truth – always. We are sincere, and we are not pushy. We have learned to manage the *drainers* in our lives and seek to be a *charger* in all our relationships. Through this we have built trust with everyone. Their view of our value and their support for us has lifted, deepening our connections.

5. Our thinking has been turned inside out!

We have learned to move from the narrow mindset of W.I.I.F.M (*What's in it for **me**?*) to the more mature and effective response W.C.I.C. (*What can I contribute?*). When we meet people, we always seek first to understand life and business from *their* perspective before we offer ours. This is now second nature to us because we know that once we have listened well, when we get to present our offering, it is contextualised and presented in a way that will best meet their needs – not ours! It means that *our* agenda is not uppermost in our minds. Instead, we are focused on helping meet *their* agenda and in doing so, we get a win for us as well.

6. We have set our True North and know what's non-negotiable.

We have learned to *read the chart* of life. We know that it is easy to end up on the rocks but we have learned to embrace those core components into our life that are both necessary and non-negotiable. These are the values that will keep our life compass pointing north. We work hard on and embrace the core values of moral integrity. We pursue truth. We show respect for others. We seek to serve them and we are accountable for all our actions. We are careful to demonstrate humility, to show authentic care for others and we are open in our communication. We understand that it is smart to quickly admit when we get things wrong or make a mistake. Because of this, we can chart a wise course, we know where we are heading and we can navigate the rocks.

7. We understand 'Heart Matters'.

We now understand the value of EQ (Emotional Intelligence) and we have learned to understand *matters of the heart*. Whether we are natural leaders or followers, there are lessons we have learned and put into practice. We understand the five stages of communication and how to connect with our bosses,' peers, families and friends. We know how they function. We don't want to be casual or destructive in any communication. We can be frivolous, but it will not make us very effective.

We know that if we engage with others using facts we are off to a good start. We may feel safer by being cautious and conservative, but we now understand that may be what causes people to hold back and resist engaging with us. Being genuine, open and sincere with our connections may leave us feeling a little vulnerable or exposed, but that openness will go a long way towards moving us from a simple relationship to a ***real**ationship*: one that goes deep, is sincere and has a *win-win* as its primary goal.

8. We learned the seven secrets of thriving team relationships.

We remember and *use people's names*. We have learnt to *listen long and talk short*, we are interested in *their* story because that gives us context. We are able to *verbalise our appreciation* for others, their work and their passion. We try hard to *stay genuinely engaged in our conversations* with others. We always *look for reasons to say thank you* and are *sincere in our praise* of them and their work and we *demonstrate our genuine care* by offering to help them.

We have learned how to identify the *competent jerks* and the *lovable fools* that work in our office, business or organisation! We know those we prefer to work with and who will make our team effective. We can now recognise the signs of a team that is conflicted. We see who gives out *blame*, the people that love being the *martyr* and we can identify those that are simply *unpleasant* to engage with. We have also tagged those that have proven themselves to be *untrustworthy*. We have learned that it is these behaviours that make our team ineffective and we have committed to use all our skills to turn our culture around.

9. We are learning to be effective, authentic and radical.

We are learning to ignore the fakes in our world and embrace only what is authentic. Living *radical lives* means swimming upstream – against the current and more often than not, doing the opposite of the crowd. We are learning and probing, seeking to understand better. We have learned to ask *what* or *how* questions - not *why* - because we know that '*why*' makes others defensive. It is these skills that make us radical, it means we will stand out from the crowd and we will be noticed.

10. We understand how quickly Shift Happens.

We have embraced the principle that *shift happens* – nothing remains the same and we are learning to embrace the speed of change, not fight it. When the wind shifts – we adjust our course to suit the prevailing conditions. We do not compromise because we have given considerable thought to the *hill on which we are willing to die*, the values that are at the core of who we are.

Nokia and Kodak are poignant examples to us of ineffective businesses. They failed to adjust to a changing market and ignored the importance of embracing fast-changing technological advances. *Authenticity* is based on who we are - not what we say.

We use the tools and ideas for managing the difficult people we meet. We now understand the strategy of *navigation by judgment and accountability through realationship*. This principle allows us to leave team members to manage the detail and make decisions based on what they see. We do hold them accountable because we are in a trusted relationship with them. (I am writing this in Vientiane, Laos, where I have just invested five days deepening our **real**ationships with six existing partners and spending time getting to know two potential new ones.) I know from personal experience these **real**ational principles really work!

11. We are willing to tack into a head wind.

We are now open to changing tack and realise that the best way to get where we wish to go is not always a direct route. We understand that life is sometimes a head wind. We have to tack into the forces that oppose us, and we will find a way to zig zag to our destination – even if we get a little wet and it takes longer than we wish.

We take a life-long perspective not a short-term grab. We are headed for Hobart and the finish line– not just the first marker. We now pace ourselves and value the deep **real**ationships we are forming on the journey. **Real**ationships that will last a lifetime. We are learning treasured lessons along the way and when we reach our goal, the lessons learned on the journey will equip us well for the next task we are assigned.

12. We are using our new skills to streak ahead.

Our spinnaker is set and we are soaring. We have embraced these 12 principles and are well along life's road to ensuring our interaction with others, at every level, is more effective, goes deeper, is powerful and positively impacting us all. We will have *set our spinnaker* and we will start to streak ahead. We will move up through the fleet and we will slowly but surely find ourselves at the front of the race. The wind will be at our back and there will be a sense of calm and peace.

The true value of **real**ationships we form, will give us a deep sense of satisfaction because we are helping others and now seeing the world from their point of view. That perspective empowers us and enables us to actually make our world a better and more engaging place in which to live.

My sincere wish for you is that you apply these principles into your own life, business and **real**ationships. You know how to set *your* spinnaker and you can soar!

SAILING

I'll not pretend I've sailed these waters well;
they've been too rough for my limited skills.

O yes, I remember days when we came down-wind
with our sails filled
slicing through blue summer seas
and feeling glad to be alive;
but all too often we spent our time
beating up-wind under stormy skies
straining every nerve and muscle
to stay on course,
tossed about in heavy seas
continually shipping water
barely managing to survive.

And now with torn tackle
and hull sprung
we lie quietly, waiting,
in this place
feeling beneath the tender touch
of shallow sands.

On deck I can still hear the distant sounds

of open sea,

but down below,

Cabined off from everything,

all is quiet;

only the feel of dry stale spray

clinging to my flesh

keeps the past alive.

> Origin unknown

Your Next Steps...

- ☐ If you found what I have written helpful, please pass these ideas and principles on to someone else and use them to help others.

- ☐ If you would like me to speak at your company conference or event, wherever you live, I would love to chat with you. Email me: rb@richardbeaumont.com.au

- ☐ If you want to consider how to engage in helping others – with some of the most amazing but poorest people on the planet, look at what the Entrust Foundation does: www.entrust.org.au

###

References:

1. **Marcus Buckingham**, author of "Nine Lies About Work" - Published by Gildan Media.

2. **Charles Sykes**, author of "Dumbing Down Our Kids" - Published by St. Martin's Griffin.

3. **Chris Voss**, author of "Never Split the Difference" – published by Random House Business Books.

4. **Mark Goulston**, author of "Just Listen" – published by Harper Collins Focus.

5. **Roy T. Bennett**, author of "The Light in the Heart" – Kindle edition.

6. **Stephen Covey**, author of "The Seven Habits of Highly Effective People" – Published by Simon & Schuster UK Ltd.

7. **Casciaro, T. & Lobo, M.** (2005). Competent Jerks, Loveable Fools, and the Formation of Social Networks. Harvard Business Review.

8. **New York Times** – 5th February 2008

About the author

Richard and his wife Julie were born in Christchurch New Zealand and moved to Australia in 1978.

They lived aboard a ship for 6 years, travelling the world as volunteers - taking quality literature to developing nations.

Richard then spent 10 years directing a not-for-profit organisation in Australia and then moved into senior business management. In 2001 he joined the Board of Entrust's parent company as a volunteer Director, then established Entrust Foundation and was appointed CEO in 2008.

Richard coaches and mentors a wide range of people, is a director of Private Philanthropic Foundations and several NFP entities. He has travelled and worked in over 85 countries and regularly visits Entrust projects in 15 nations throughout Africa, India and Asia.

His passion is to help *"Uplift the ultra-poor"* in any way he can. He is a business professional, consultant, coach, engaging speaker, published author, a REALationship specialist, a community development facilitator, and advisor to some of Australia's high-net-worth families.

He continues to travel widely, loves sailing and has no plans to slow down any time soon!

www.ingramcontent.com/pod-product-compliance
Lightning Source LLC
Chambersburg PA
CBHW050311010526
44107CB00055B/2188